1993

Doug

I understand you're interested in books about WW1, so I hope this book is one you don't have and will provide more information f

Thanks again for being the be

boss anyone could ask for - it h

been a great 2 years!!

Tabby (alias Lois)

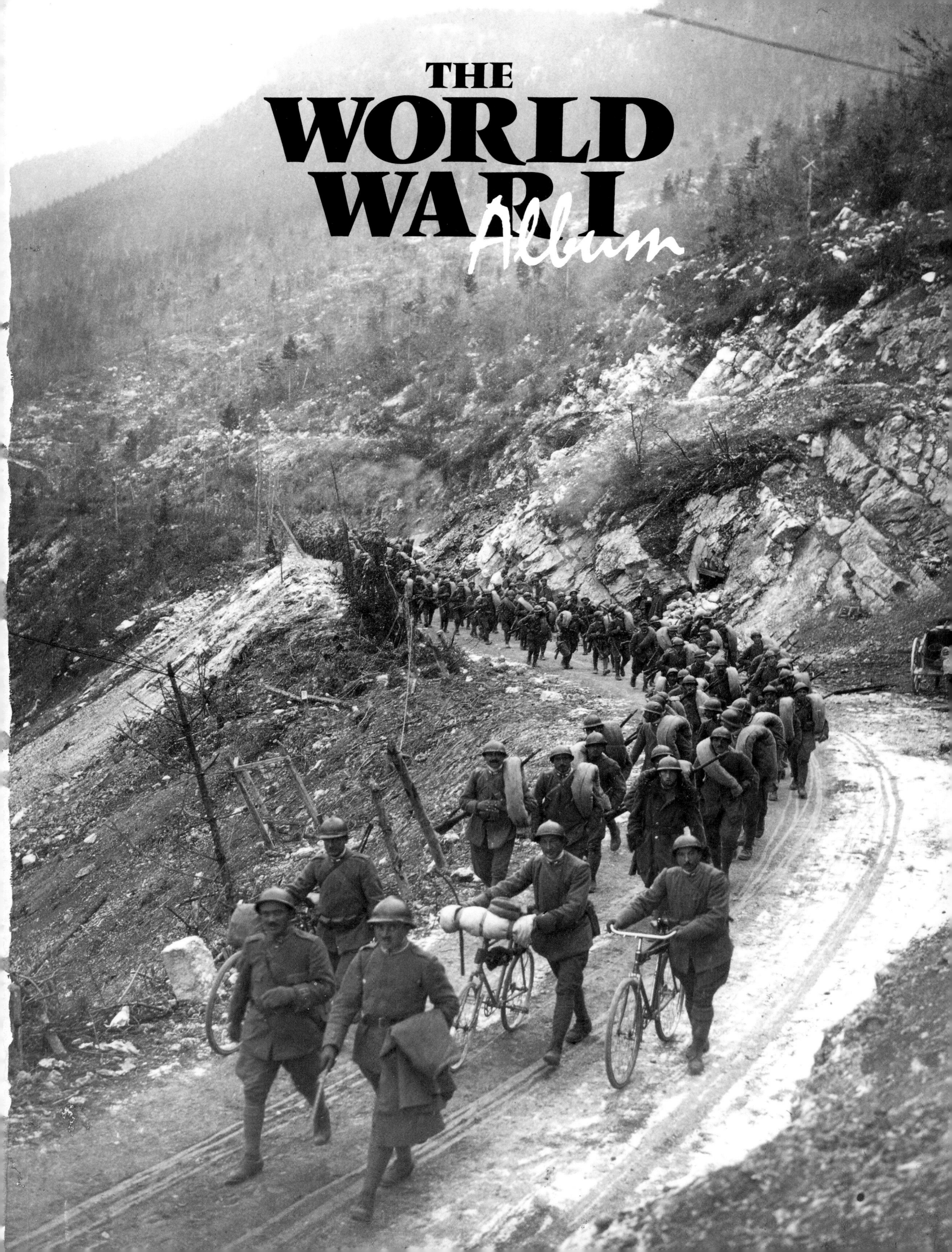
THE
WORLD
WAR I
Album

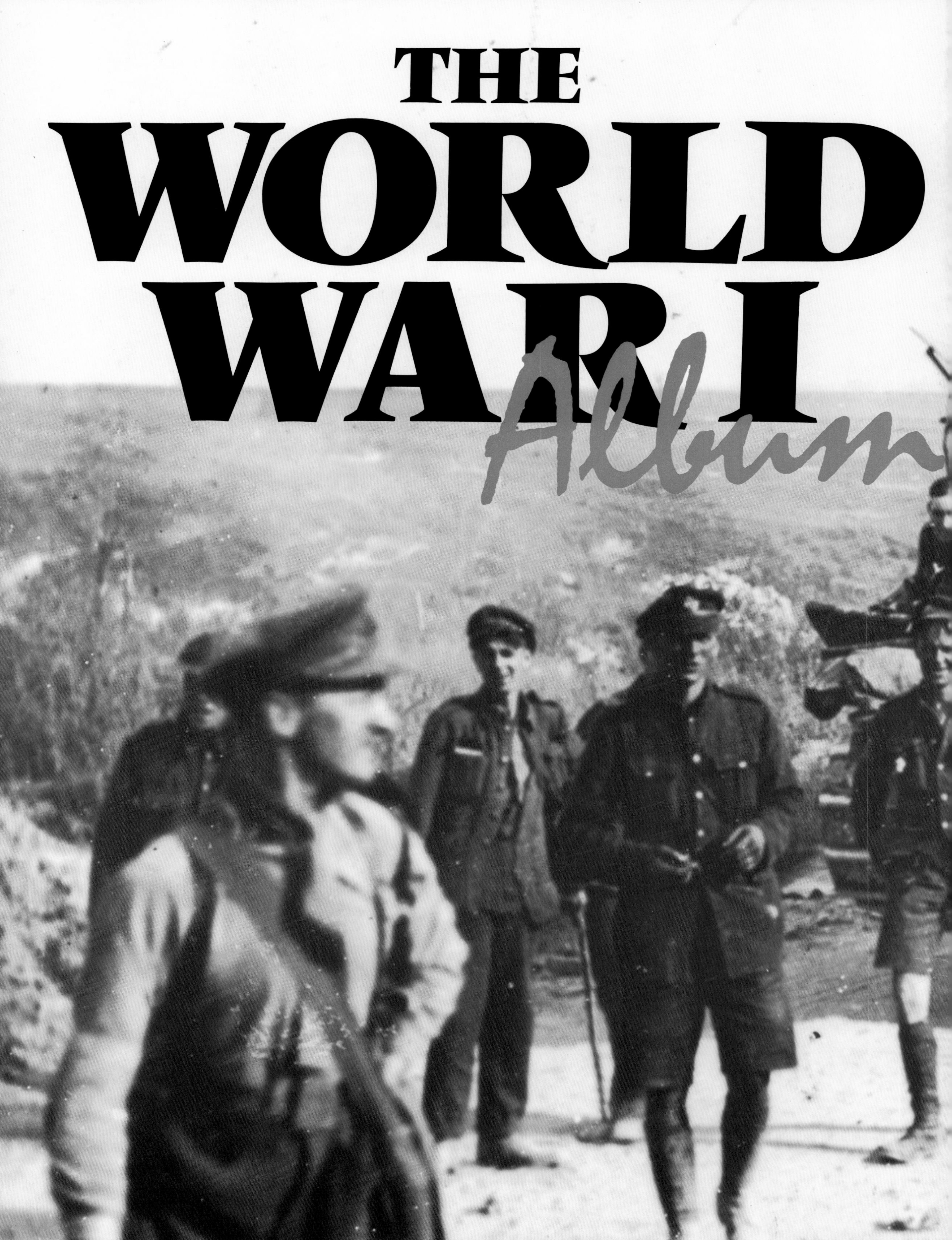
THE
WORLD
WAR I
Album

5
SMITHMARK

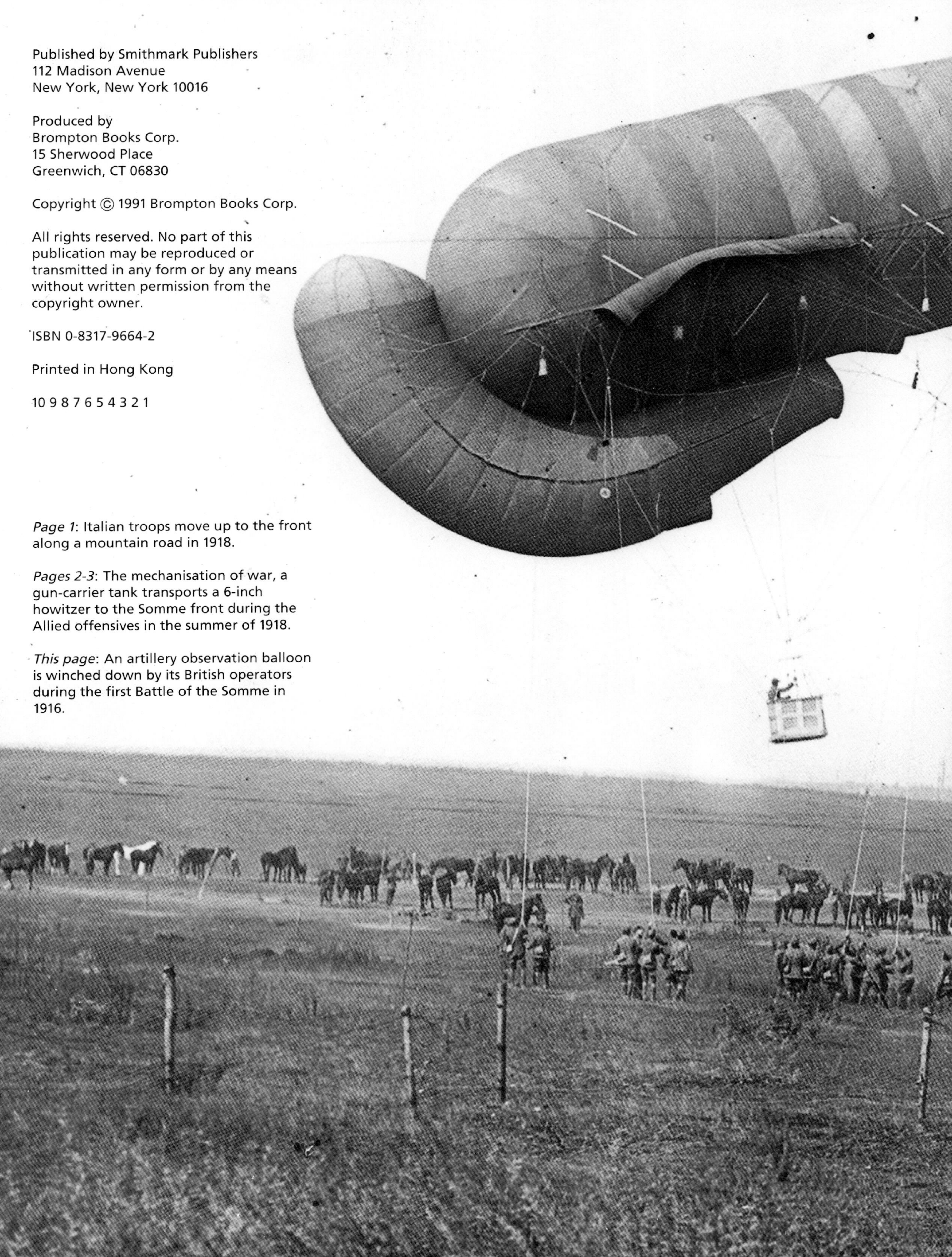

Published by Smithmark Publishers
112 Madison Avenue
New York, New York 10016

Produced by
Brompton Books Corp.
15 Sherwood Place
Greenwich, CT 06830

ISBN 0-8317-9664-2

Printed in Hong Kong

10 9 8 7 6 5 4 3 2 1

Page 1: Italian troops move up to the front along a mountain road in 1918.

Pages 2-3: The mechanisation of war, a gun-carrier tank transports a 6-inch howitzer to the Somme front during the Allied offensives in the summer of 1918.

This page: An artillery observation balloon is winched down by its British operators during the first Battle of the Somme in 1916.

CONTENTS

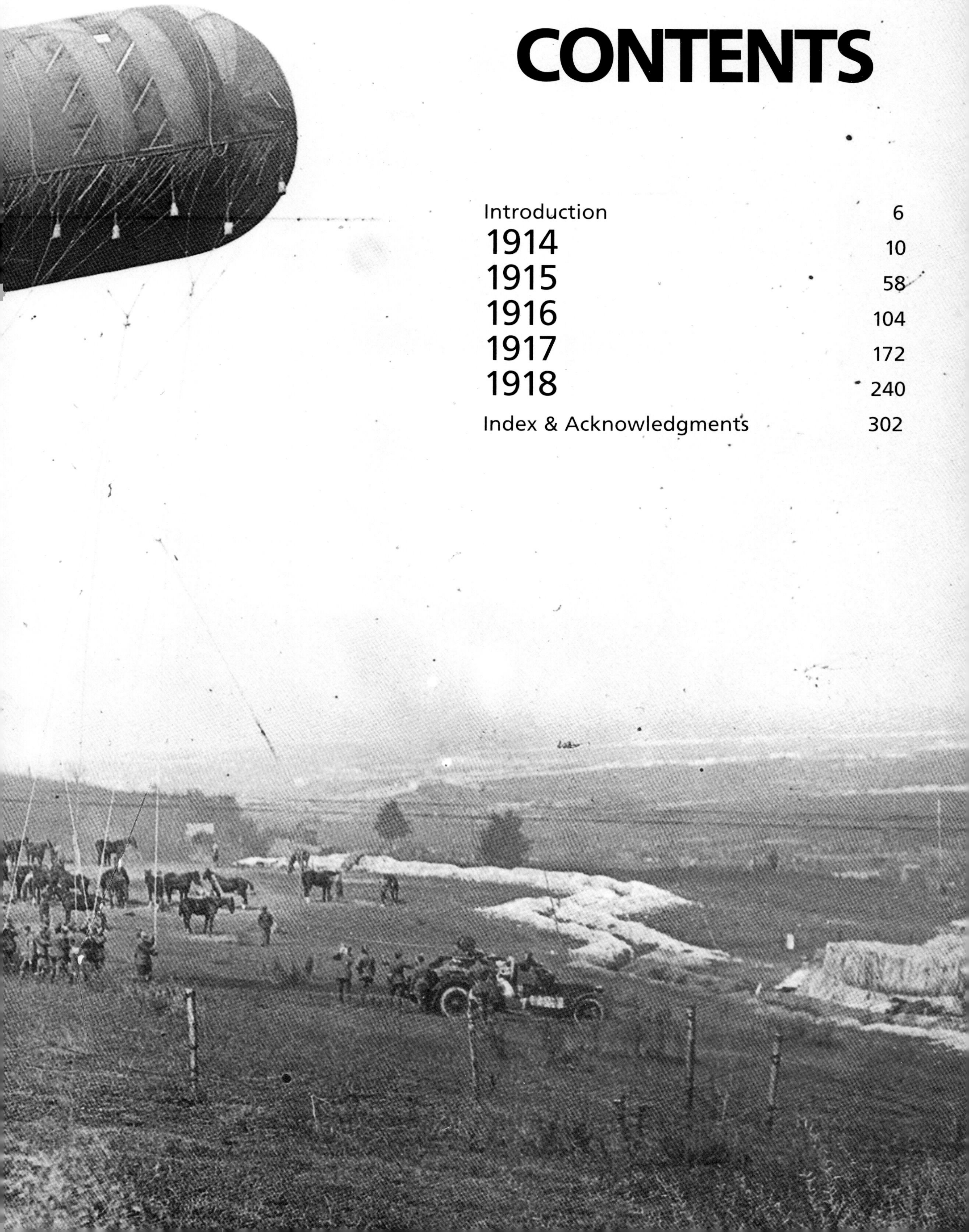

INTRODUCTION

On 28 June 1914 the assassination of the heir to the Austro-Hungarian Empire at Sarajevo set the stage for a global conflict diplomats and dynasties alike had said would never happen.

But the holocaust that followed was all too real. Within weeks of Archduke Ferdinand's death, Europe was mobilising to fight the War to end all Wars – a war that would leave at least nine million dead and change the face of the globe.

The Great War, as World War I was known, was the first Europe-wide conflict for nearly a century. Prior to its outbreak, a system of alliances, each delicately balanced, had sufficed to keep the peace. This balance of power relied on opposing forces being roughly equal in strength: any imbalance would not only prove fatal to at least one of the combatants but could also bring the whole of the continent – and thereafter the world – into conflict.

Events took just six weeks to unfold after the incident at Sarajevo. Heir to the Austrian throne, the Archduke had come to the province of Bosnia, seized by Austria in 1908 and today part of modern Yugoslavia. The Bosnians were Serbs, and understandably strove to unite with the neighboring country of Serbia, then independent under Russian protection, in a single state.

The Serbians were blamed by Austria for the assassination, even though student Gavrilo Princip was technically a Bosnian. One month after the fatal bullet, on 28 July 1914, Austria and Serbia were at war.

Serbia's chief ally, Russia, called up her armies in readiness – a move that alarmed Germany, which had always considered mighty Russia its principal potential adversary. Seeing the bear waking from its slumber, Germany determined to avoid the nightmare of a war on two fronts by eliminating Russia's ally France on the west before turning east to face the mightier opponent. But access to France was best achieved through neutral Belgium – and the German advance there, intended to outflank French defenses, was met with an ultimatum from Britain. The choice was war or withdrawal . . . and on 4 August Britain joined the rest of Europe in taking up arms.

Underlying causes are with hindsight easy to see – and were as much economic as political. With the Industrial Revolution, the search was on for markets in which to sell its products, and with new colonies in short supply disputes over African and Asian territories pointed to larger conflicts ahead. Besides, Germany had failed to gather as many colonies as Britain, France and the rest, having only come into existence in 1871 as the union of 35 states forged in the 1870 Franco-Prussian War.

Kaiser Wilhelm II, a relative of Queen Victoria, lacked the statesmanlike qualities to rein in the overweening ambition that sprang from envy. Treaties so carefully constructed by Chancellor Bismarck were removed, and old allies like Russia alienated, while the construction of a capable fleet alarmed Britain, hitherto the unchallenged European sea power. The tinder of suspicion, smouldering for decades, was fanned into violent life: Germany was ready to test her strength, and three decades of covert construction and economic growth saw her in a position to enter the superpower stage on more than equal terms.

Elsewhere, the old order was changing with the establishment of new countries like Albania and Serbia, Bulgaria, Rumania and Greece. The Ottoman Empire (Turkey) and the Austro-Hungarian Empire were crumbling at the edges – and Austria took Archduke Ferdinand's assassination as its cue to reverse the process.

Surrounded as she was by potential adversaries, Germany's best chance of achieving gains, or so her leaders believed, was a pre-emptive strike – but the Schlieffen Plan was a hopeless gamble. The diplomatic chess game had gone horribly wrong, and it was the old alliances of Germany and Austro-Hungary, Britain, France and Russia that lined up like pawns.

World War I saw technology progress at an unparalleled rate, bringing aircraft, tanks and the submarine, to name but three innovations, into the vocabulary of warfare for the first time. Tactics for these and other new weapons had to be devised 'on the hoof', but it was certain that never again would cavalry sweep the battlefield nor surface ships supply armies with impunity. Yet the greatest carnage of all was to take place in the trenches: Verdun, the Somme and Passchendaele were names that passed into the language as symbolic of massive waste of life.

Verdun survived a ten-month German bombardment – the longest ever in the history of warfare – but at the cost of 700,000 lives overall, while British losses at the Somme were the greatest of any wartime army to date. This was not to be the War to end all Wars – but it was to be the last war to be fought with a crippling mixture of nineteenth and twentieth century tactics and technology.

World War I was the culmination of a number of disparate factors, set off by a single incident and settled only after four years of desperate fighting in the most inhuman of conditions. The men who set off in 1914 did so with the message ringing in their ears that they'd be 'home by Christmas'. They were not told which one . . .

Previous page: Battleships of the British 5th Battle Squadron open fire on the German forces at the Battle of Jutland.

Above: Two tokens of the changed times during World War I – an aircraft factory mass-producing what had recently been a rare novelty and women doing work that before the war would have been an entirely male preserve.

Left: Admiral Jackie Fisher had led the transformation in the British Navy in the years before 1914 which had seen its forces concentrated in European waters to face the German challenge.

Right: From left, General Joffre, French C-in-C, President Poincare, King George V, General Foch, and General Haig, British C-in-C, in August 1916. Relations between the Allies were often less amicable than this photo suggests.

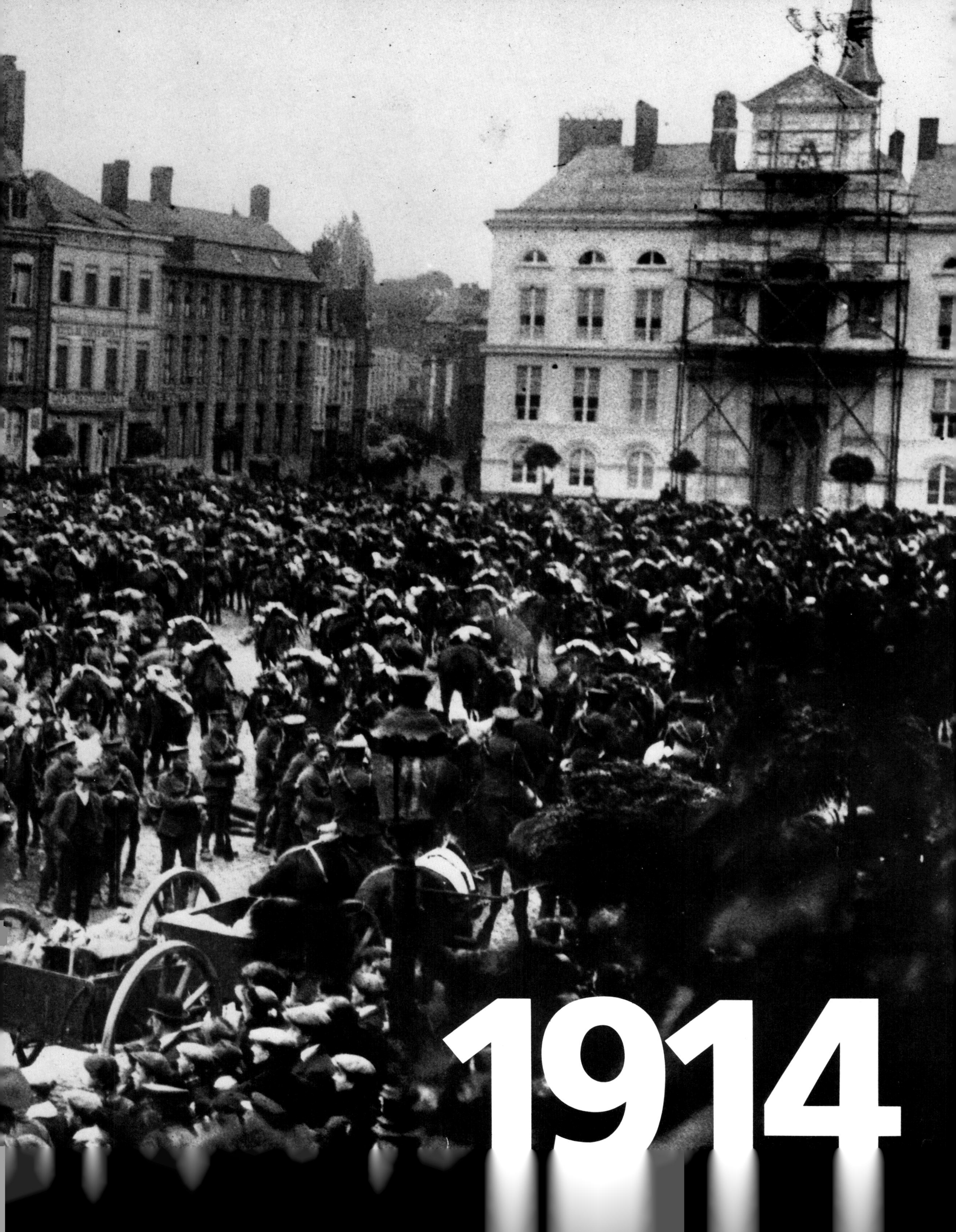

1914

The fated drive of Archduke Franz Ferdinand and his wife through Sarajevo on 28 June was punctuated by incident: a bomb had earlier been thrown at them but had missed. When 19-year-old Gavrilo Princip mounted the running board to shoot the Archduke at point-blank range, the fuse had been well and truly lit for conflict on a global scale.

A domino effect saw nations queuing to make war: Austria-Hungary declared war on Serbia on 28 July, Germany declaring war on Russia three days later on 1 August. Austria-Hungary declared war on Russia on 6 August and Serbia declared war on Germany.

Having declared war on France on 3 August, Germany wasted no time in invading neutral Belgium the following day. The intention was to knock France out of the war within six weeks by attacking through her undefended border with Belgium. The German spearhead would then complete a great arc and pin the French against their own defenses on the German border. Caught in this powerful pincer movement, the French Army would surely crumble, leaving the Germans free to concentrate on the Russian menace from the east.

Britain had other ideas, declaring war on Germany and beginning a naval blockade. This was followed by the embarkation of the British Expeditionary Force, comprising a total of 110,000 men in one cavalry and four infantry divisions, which had landed in France by the 17th and straightaway reinforced the retreating French. Belgium's much-trumpeted fortifications had proved no match for the German artillery, while French troops met with a series of setbacks at Morhange and Sarrebourg after they initially followed Plan XVII, a tactical straitjacket even more misguided than Germany's Schlieffen Plan that involved in the event a short-lived incursion into Alsace.

The Germans, having advanced a long way in a short time before being repulsed in the Battle of the Marne in September, prudently withdrew to rest and re-arm in the safety of defensive trenches along the River Aisne. The Allies dug positions parallel to the German trenches, establishing a pattern of warfare that would last for the next four years. By mid October, both sides had dug trenches from the Swiss border to the English Channel.

This hitherto unknown form of warfare was to pose real problems to forces whose tactics had been formulated on the basis of rapid movement on the battlefield under covering fire, troops advancing in turn until a final, glorious bayonet charge secured victory. But this was not the Napoleonic Wars, and things were to change quickly. First and most noticeably uniforms became drab khaki or gray for all ranks: the brighter the color the more assistance enemy snipers were given. Machine guns, hand grenades and spades were the order of the day for the infantry, who huddled in their trenches as the artillery barrage blazed overhead.

War had broken out on the Eastern Front on 17 August when the Russians attacked East Prussia. Their offensive was particularly timely for the Allies, since it caused the diversion of many German troops from France to defend their

country's eastern frontier. The Russian army, though large in size, was clearly going to be no match for the well organised and equipped Germans – as was apparent on 29 August at Tannenberg where the Russian Second Army was completely destroyed and some 120,000 prisoners taken. The Russians would fare better against Austria whose initial assault on Serbia earlier in August had been repelled with some ease. The Austrian loss of Galicia to Ivanoff's army group led to Germany lending further aid to their ally – already confirmed a liability.

Back on the Western Front, the Battle of Ypres which started on 1 October was won by the indomitable strength of the British infantry. General von Falkenhayn, a recent replacement for the ineffective Chief of Staff Moltke, had determined that one last, desperate German assault could catch the Allies unawares: as it was, the inexperienced reserve troops he threw in were easy pickings for the BEF's guns. Ypres stood between the Germans and the Channel Ports, and the triangle of Béthune, Armentières and Ypres was to prove a killing ground for both sides.

Casualties in the First Battle of Ypres were extensive: the already depleted British lost 50,000 – the remnants of the old pre-war British Army – while for the Germans, who thrust their recruits into the heat of battle too soon, it was the Slaughter of the Innocents. Having failed to break through, the Germans were now facing their nightmare scenario – a war on two fronts against a combination of nations with far greater manpower than their own resources.

Britain's declaration of war against Turkey on 5 November followed that country's decision to side with Germany. With the Ottoman (Turkish) Empire straddling the Middle East, it posed a clear threat both to the strategically vital Suez Canal and the oilfields of Mesopotamia. It was in an attempt to protect the latter that Indian troops took the Arabian Gulf port of Basra, but an attempt to push the Turks from the Suez Canal by a force pushing north from Sinai was less successful.

Sea power had hitherto played no great part in the conduct of the war, but the Battle of the Falklands served notice that all this was to change. Vice-Admiral Maximilian von Spee's East Asiatic Squadron consisting of the heavy cruisers *Scharnhorst* and *Gneisenau* and three light cruisers had ended up off the coast of South America where two British cruisers were sunk off Cape Coronel. The Royal Navy redressed the balance, sinking the entire German force bar one light cruiser in the Battle of the Falklands on 8 December. Although an emphatic victory, the British force sent by Admiral Fisher, had been far superior and it was no real test of strength.

November and December of 1914 saw fierce fighting in Poland, where the Germans forced a Russian retreat. The first months of the war ended in the trenches of the Western Front with a Christmas truce, weapons being laid down in favor of soccer matches, conversations and community singing. The high commands on both sides gave orders that such scenes were not to be repeated in future.

Previous page: Crowds of townspeople turn out to watch British troops moving up to the front through Ypres, October 1914.

Left: Belgian troops defend a road barricade outside Louvain, August 1914.

Right: The start of trench warfare; a sector of the front held by the British Royal Lancaster Regiment in November.

Far right: General Joffre (left) the French Chief of Staff in 1914, with General Foch, one of his leading subordinates.

Below: Count Alfred von Schlieffen, Chief of the German General Staff from 1891 to 1905, whose strategically inflexible plan involving the invasion of France – ignoring both the Russian threat and Belgium's neutrality – ensured a global conflict was inevitable.

Right: German Chancellor von Bethmann-Hollweg. Germany's political naivety in not predicting the outcome of the Schlieffen Plan was to prove her undoing.

Center right: French President Raymond Poincaré. His nation's adherence to the simplistic Plan XVII, to advance on two fronts into Lorraine and Alsace, resulted in the loss of some of the Army's finest soldiers.

Far right: King George V. Britain's entry into the war was assured when the Germans violated Belgium's neutrality of which Britain, among others, had been a guarantor.

Below right: The German Army in new field gray uniforms, 1914. Both sides had learned the lesson that different uniforms for officers and other ranks made life easy for snipers, less distinctive epaulettes or cap bands thenceforth distinguishing the ranks.

Литографія Т-ва И. Д. Сытина. Москва. 1914.

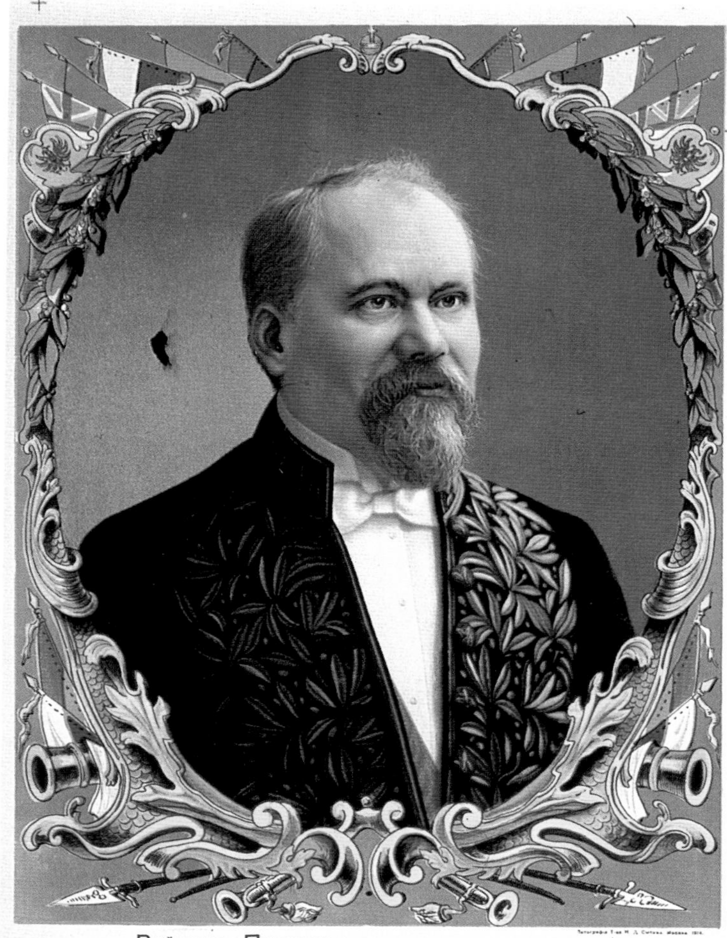

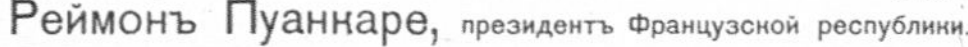

Реймонъ Пуанкаре, президентъ Французской республики.

Литографія Т-ва И. Д. Сытина. Москва. 1914.

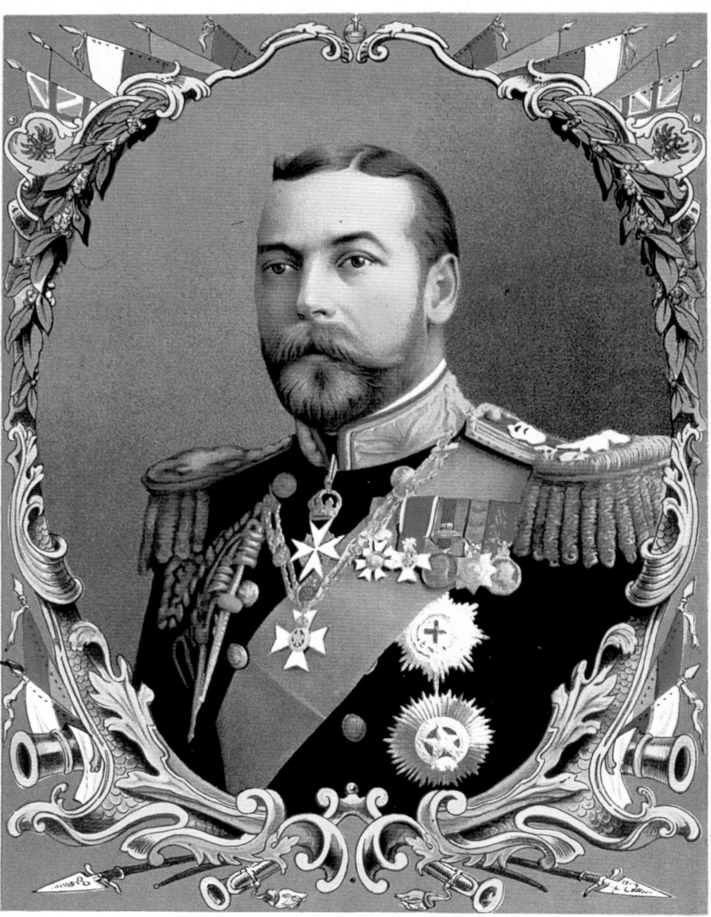

Его величество Георгъ V, король Великобританіи.

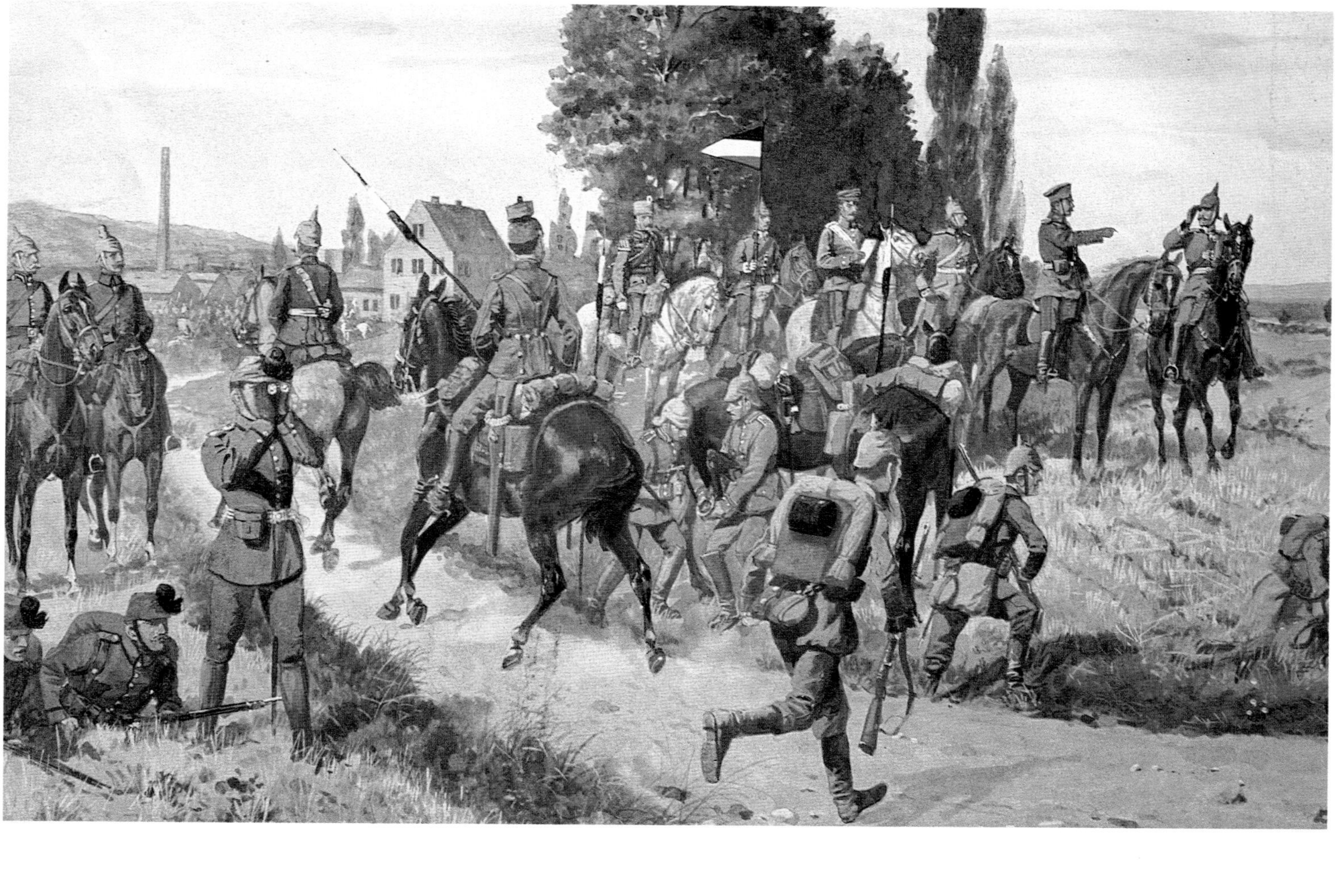

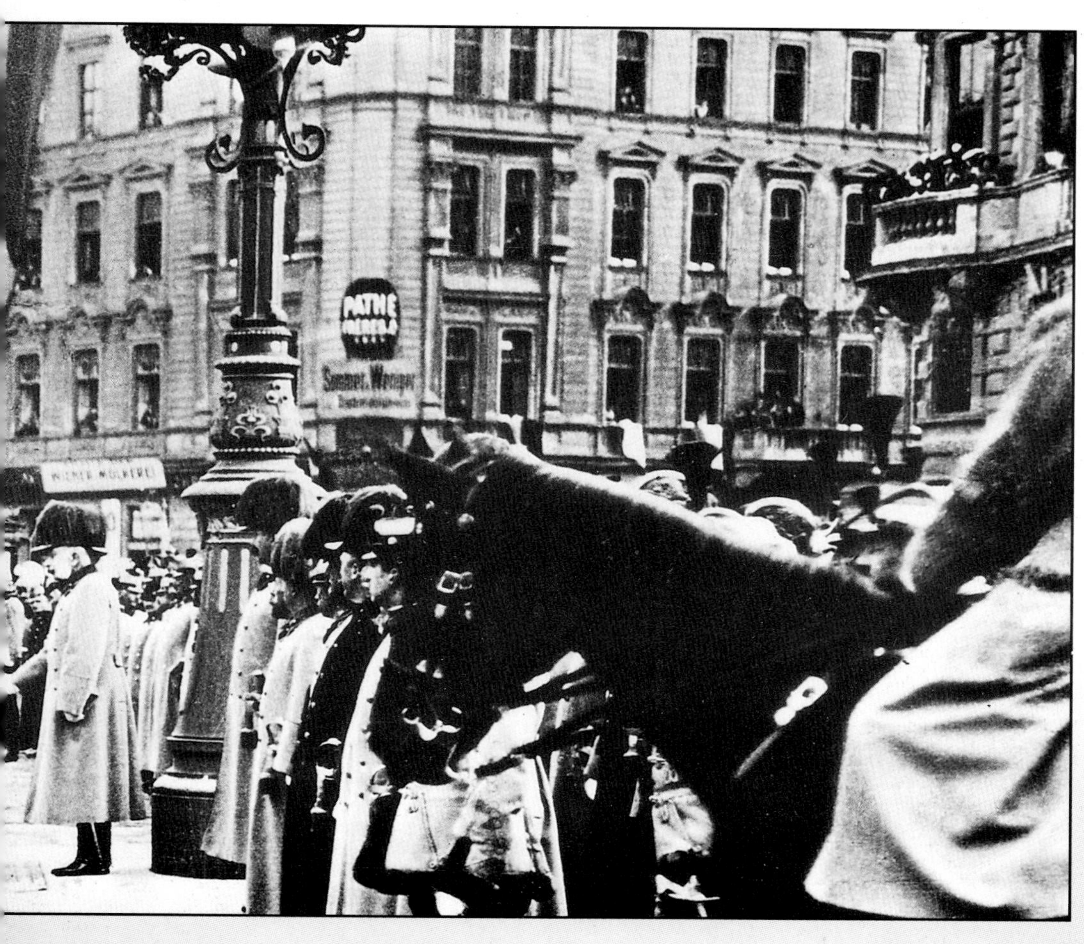

Below: German maneuvers in 1913. Cavalry played an important part in the early war, but the advent of the tank on the Somme in 1916 emphatically spelled the end of horseback warfare.

Left: Austrians on parade. Their declaration of war on neighboring Serbia, blaming them for the assassination of heir to the throne Archduke Ferdinand, was the spark that set Europe ablaze.

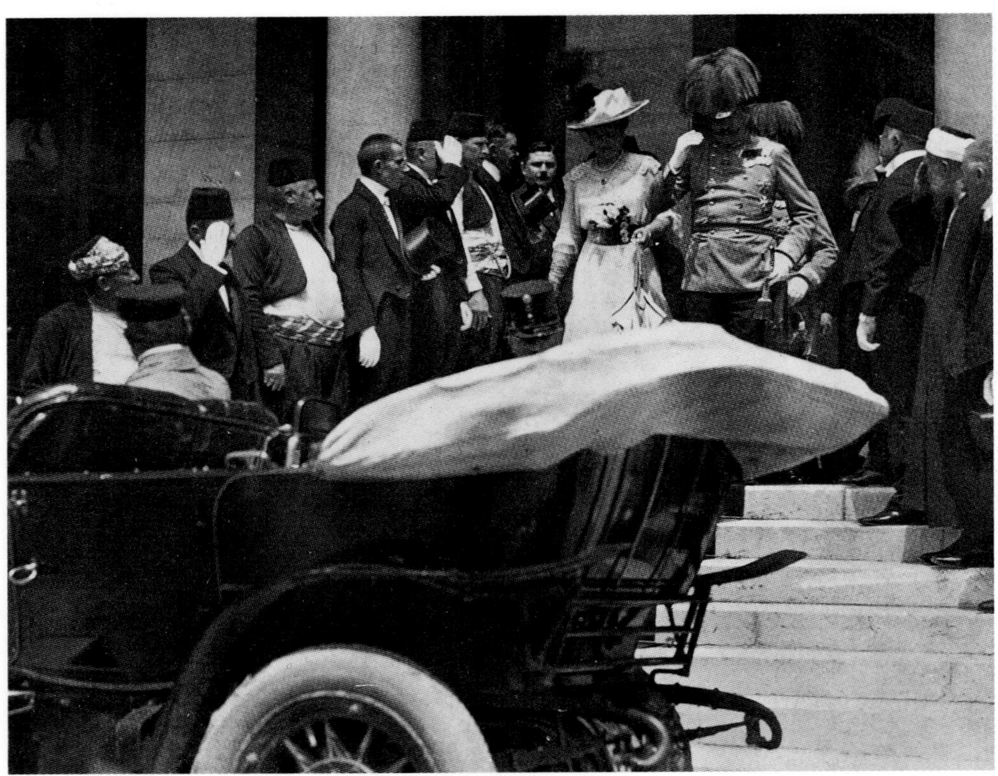

Right: The Archduke Franz Ferdinand and his wife prepare to drive through waiting crowds in an open-topped car, just minutes before a bullet delivered by 19-year-old Gavrilo Princip ended his life in the Bosnian capital, Sarajevo.

Below: The arrest of Princip, 28 June 1914. Concrete footprints now mark the spot where the Bosnian student stood to shoot the Archduke – the killer who became a national hero. The Bosnians resented Austrian rule, preferring to ally with neighboring Serbia.

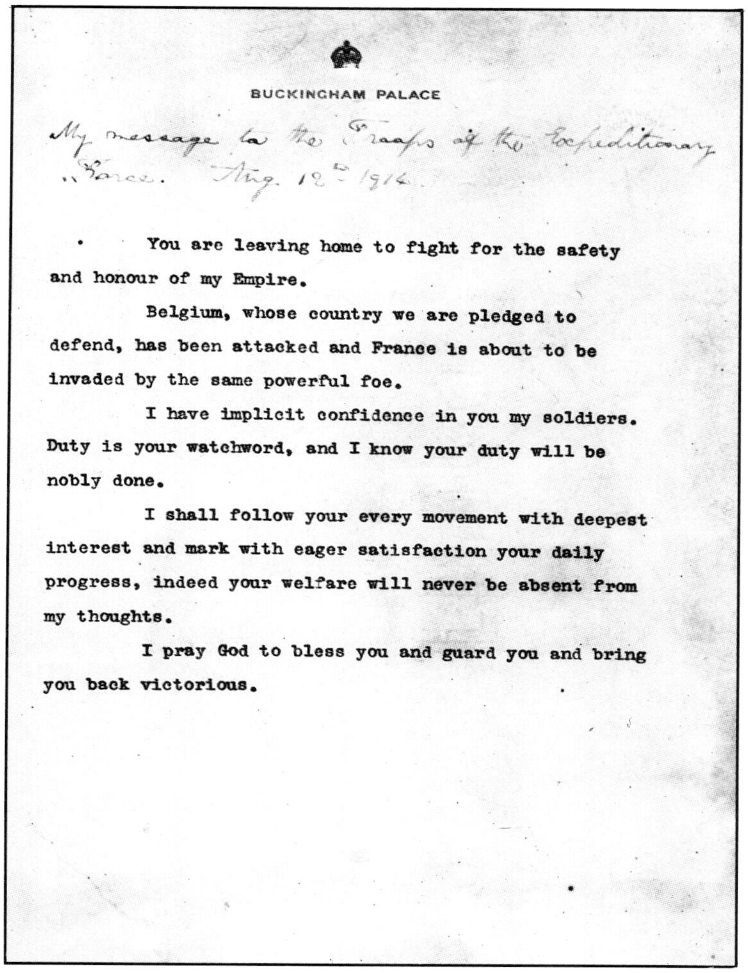

BUCKINGHAM PALACE

My message to the Troops of the Expeditionary Force. Aug. 12th 1914.

You are leaving home to fight for the safety and honour of my Empire.

Belgium, whose country we are pledged to defend, has been attacked and France is about to be invaded by the same powerful foe.

I have implicit confidence in you my soldiers. Duty is your watchword, and I know your duty will be nobly done.

I shall follow your every movement with deepest interest and mark with eager satisfaction your daily progress, indeed your welfare will never be absent from my thoughts.

I pray God to bless you and guard you and bring you back victorious.

Left: King George V's personal message to the troops of the Expeditionary Force, issued from Buckingham Palace on 12 August 1914.

Below: Recruits answered Kitchener's call in their hundreds of thousands; these men wait at the Whitehall Recruiting Office, 1914.

SPÉCIALITÉ POUR GARÇONS & FILLETTES
MAISON HENRY
35
AU PRINTEMPS
AU PRINTEMPS
TÉLÉPHONE 9883

Top left: Lacking modern arms and equipment, the poorly trained Belgian Army retreated northwards to Antwerp after the fall of Brussels on 20 August 1914. Antiquated dog-drawn machine guns are pictured during the retreat.

Bottom left: German horse-drawn transport passes through the Boulevard Baudouin during the occupation of Brussels, 26 August 1914. Largely on the initiative of Britain's First Lord of the Admiralty (navy minister) Winston Churchill, the Royal Naval Division was deployed to assist the Belgians.

Above: British Marines fill water bottles, Ostend, August 1914.

Right: Officers of the 1st Cameronians consult before the Battle of Le Cateau, 25 August 1914. Le Cateau proved one of several costly holding actions fought as the BEF withdrew southwards to the Marne.

Left: A surprisingly well-dug French trench, September 1914.

Below: Men of the Queen's Bays guard German prisoners (Death's Head Hussars) after the action at Nery, 1 September 1914.

Right: Major H Harvey-Kelly of the Royal Flying Corps (on right of picture studying a map) was the first British pilot to land in France after the declaration of war, landing at Amiens in the BE 2A pictured. He was killed behind the German lines on 29 April 1917.

347

Left: French cavalrymen escort an important convoy of German prisoners following the Battle of the Marne. Fought in September 1914, the battle was a rare triumph for the French.

Above: French troops hold the bank of a canal on the Western Front, 29 September 1914.

Right: The Military Governor of Paris, General Joseph Galliéni, whose call for an attack on the exposed right flank of the German First Army proved decisive in securing victory at the Marne.

Below: French troops storm into Alsace in fulfilment of the doomed Plan XVII. Their only gain was a small amount of German territory near Mulhouse, the operation having no bearing on the course of the war.

Above: The rapid and effective German artillery was a major factor in the swift occupation of Belgium. A 21cm howitzer is pictured.

Left: Crown Prince Rupprecht, commander of the German Sixth Army. After initial success in the battles of Morhange and Sarrebourg, Rupprecht's aggressive tactics could not prevent defeat at the Marne.

Right: Nicknamed 'Big Bertha', Germany's devastating 42cm howitzers, built at the Krupp armament factory, proved a key element in the destruction of Belgian forts at Liège and Namur, along with their smaller 30.5cm sisters.

AUX HABITANTS
DE LA
VILLE de LILLE

I. — L'armée allemande ne fait la guerre qu'aux armées françaises, anglaises et belges, pas à la population qui ne prend pas part à la guerre. Elle garantit aux citoyens toutes leurs propriétés, pourvu qu'on ne commette pas d'actes d'hostilité contre les troupes allemandes.

II. — Afin que la population soit tranquille, seront pris comme otages :

Mgr **CHAROST**, Evêque de Lille;
MM. **TRÉPONT**, Préfet du Nord;
DELORY, Député du Nord;
GHESQUIÈRE, Député du Nord;
DELSALLE, Maire de Lille;
CRÉPY-SAINT-LÉGER, **REMY**, **LIÉGEOIS-SIX**, **DUBURCQ**, **BOUDON**, **BRUCKERS D'HUGO**,
Adjoints, et tous les Conseillers municipaux.

Ces otages devront se présenter à la Mairie, chaque jour, à 10 heures du matin (heure française), 11 heures (heure allemande).

L'autorité militaire se réserve le droit de choisir d'autres otages.

III. — Le Maire doit déposer demain la somme de cinq millions de francs comme cautionnement. Cette somme sera rendue à la Ville si la population se montre raisonnable et ne commet aucun acte d'hostilité. La question de la contribution de guerre sera réglée plus tard par l'autorité militaire allemande.

IV. — Il y a grand danger à toucher aux obus non éclatés qui seront trouvés dans la ville. La population doit indiquer à la Mairie les endroits où on en trouvera.

V. — Je désire que la vie régulière commence aussi vite que possible, que l'industrie et le commerce ne soient pas interrompus, que la police garde ses fonctions. Les cultivateurs des environs pourront entrer librement dans la ville, comme d'ordinaire.

J'espère que des relations correctes s'établiront entre la population et les soldats allemands.

VI. — Tout ce que l'autorité allemande reçoit et tout ce que les soldats demanderont pour leur propre usage, sera payé comptant ; au besoin, une taxe sera établie par une commission spéciale.

Toute réquisition est interdite.

LILLE, le 14 Octobre 1914.

WAHNSCHAFFE.
Général-Major.

"Bulletin de Lille"

Top left: This 42cm howitzer shell bears ironic greetings from the German gun crew to France's General Joffre.

Left: A poster issued by the Germans in an attempt to persuade the citizens of Lille to co-operate with the invading forces who, it claims, 'only make war against the French, British and Belgian armies'. Nonetheless it also announces that hostages are to be taken from among the town's prominent public figures as a guarantee of good behavior.

Above: The reign of Germany's Chief of General Staff Colonel General Helmut von Moltke ended on 14 September when he was replaced by General Erich von Falkenhayn. His demise coincided with that of the fated Schlieffen Plan, defeated and discredited at the Battle of the Marne.

Top right: General Alexander von Kluck (in cape) and his staff, 1914. As commander of the German First Army, he controlled the right wing of the push through Belgium.

Bottom right: Civilian cars are requisitioned for French Army use, Paris, August 1914. The taxis of Paris were used to rush troops to the front for the battle that would become known as the 'miracle of the Marne.'

Left: On the outbreak of war, Britain was indisputably the world's leading naval power. The principal ships were the 'Dreadnought' battleships but older ships were still important. HMS *Lord Nelson*, a pre-Dreadnought type, is pictured in 1914.

Above: The transformation of the British Navy into a force of modern ships concentrated in European waters was led by Admiral Sir John 'Jackie' Fisher.

Right: Admiral Sir Percy Scott who, when a Captain, combined with Admiral Fisher to modernize and raise the standards of Royal Navy gunnery, long in decline.

Below: HMS *Iron Duke, Marlborough* and an unknown *King George V* - class vessel arrive off Spithead July 1914, for a trial mobilisation which became real with the approach of war.

Left: German naval might masses in the recently-completed Kiel Canal. The Kriegsmarine had grown steadily under Admiral von Tirpitz and, while still inferior in number to the Royal Navy, was by 1914 a force to be reckoned with.

Above: Further proof that the Imperial German Navy was building in strength even before the war: these ships in line astern are headed by the flagship *Preussen* and contain *Pommern, Lothringen, Hannover, Schlesien* and others.

Right: The German battleship *Kronprinz* under construction. The strategy of building large and expensive capital ships in imitation of the Royal Navy was not to prove enormously successful.

Below: HMS *Audacious* is sunk by a mine off the north coast of Ireland. One of the earliest victims of this cheap and effective anti-shipping weapon on 27 October 1914, the battleship was one of the Royal Navy's latest acquisitions.

Top left: French President Raymond Poincaré arrives in Petrograd, Russia, in July 1914. The Germans much feared Russian involvement in the war, though early actions against the ill-organized Russian Army were remarkably successful.

Bottom left: The Russian Army mobilises, 1914. With a peacetime strength of one million swelled to four million after full mobilisation, it was crucial for the Germans that they successfully completed the invasion of France before the Russian threat became a tangible one.

Above: Russian prisoners in German captivity on the Eastern Front, 1914. The German Eighth Army captured some 120,000 Russians at Tannenberg in August when routing their Second Army, going on to retake East Prussia in the Battle of the Masurian Lakes.

Right: Captured Russian soldiers are marched to the rear, 17 November 1914. Although they found some success against the less than combative Austrians, the Russians were pushed back to the Vistula in late November by a German counter-attack around Lodz led by General von Mackensen.

Top left: Street fighting in East Prussia, 1914. Intended to divert German troops from the Western Front at French request, the Russian invasion was to prove both costly and short-lived.

Bottom left: Russians fight Turks in a battle in the Caucasus. A Turkish offensive in the last days of 1914 helped bring about the Dardanelles campaign because the Russians appealed for British and French help. Despite these worries, the Turks were badly defeated by mid January 1915.

Above: A 7.62mm PM1910 Russian machine gun, mounted on a motorcycle combination and used in an anti-aircraft role.

Right: Czar Nicholas II, who was very much involved in Russian strategy and tactics of the war alongside his commanders.

Above: A Russian battery is prepared for action against the Austrian fortress of Przemysl during the Galician campaign of late 1914.

Left: General Pavel Rennenkampf, commander of the Russian First Army, pictured in August 1914. Unfortunately for the Russian war effort, Rennenkampf had poor relations with his own chief of staff as well as with fellow General Samsonov, commanding the Second Army.

Top right: Russian troops of the First Army march through a German town in East Prussia during the early days of their offensive.

Bottom right: An Austro-Hungarian artillery battery is prepared for action in defense of a mountain village.

Left: Rear-Admiral Ernest Troubridge commanded a cruiser force which might have intercepted the *Goeben* during her voyage to Turkey. He was acquitted by a court martial afterwards because his orders were vague but only had shore appointments thereafter.

Right: German military adviser General Liman von Sanders, commander of the successful Turkish forces at Gallipoli. He had earlier been instrumental in bringing Turkey into the war.

Below: The German battlecruiser *Goeben*, which with its crew, was transferred to the Turkish Navy on its arrival in the Dardanelles in August 1914. Turkey had not yet joined the war and the *Goeben* would be used by a faction within the Turkish armed forces to provoke a conflict with Russia in October.

Above: The ex-German light cruiser *Breslau* which, along with the *Goeben*, was employed by the Turks in bombarding Russian Black Sea ports on 29 October 1914. Russia declared war three days later.

Right: HMS *Gloucester* commanded by Captain Howard Kelly, RN, shadowed the *Goeben* during its escape through the Mediterranean to Turkey until ordered to turn back.

Below: The *Goeben* at anchor off Stenia in the Bosphorus.

Top left: Great enthusiasm at Dunkirk harbor on the arrival of the two Naval Brigades of the Royal Naval Division, 5 October 1914.

Bottom left: Packed inside and out, this was the last Allied train to leave Antwerp unscathed: the next one was attacked by German forces and most of the troops were captured, 9 October 1914.

Top: Indian troops, the first colonial forces to arrive in France to bolster the British Expeditionary Force, are trained to use bayonets early in the conflict. Britain and France both made full use of troops from their overseas colonies.

Above: An Indian machine gun section pictured with pack mules carrying machine gun and ammunition at Hollebeke, near Ypres, 1914.

Right: General Sir Horace Smith-Dorrien, commander of the British Second Army, who was replaced in late April 1915 for having the temerity to suggest a limited withdrawal from Ypres.

Left: Royal Naval Reservists pictured in the streets of Vieux Dieu, an eastern suburb of Antwerp, 6 October 1914.

Below left: Soldiers of the 129th Baluchis in the trenches on the outskirts of Wytschaete, October 1914. When the Germans dug trenches at the River Aisne in September the Allies followed suit, within a month creating two parallel defense lines from Switzerland to the Channel.

Right: Congestion in Thielt Marketplace during the passage of the 7th Division, 12/13 October 1914. In the center of the square is the transport of the 2nd Scots Guards.

Below: British troops advance across a field in the run-up to the First Battle of Ypres, where the resolution of the Allies in the face of uneven odds won the admiration of the Kaiser himself.

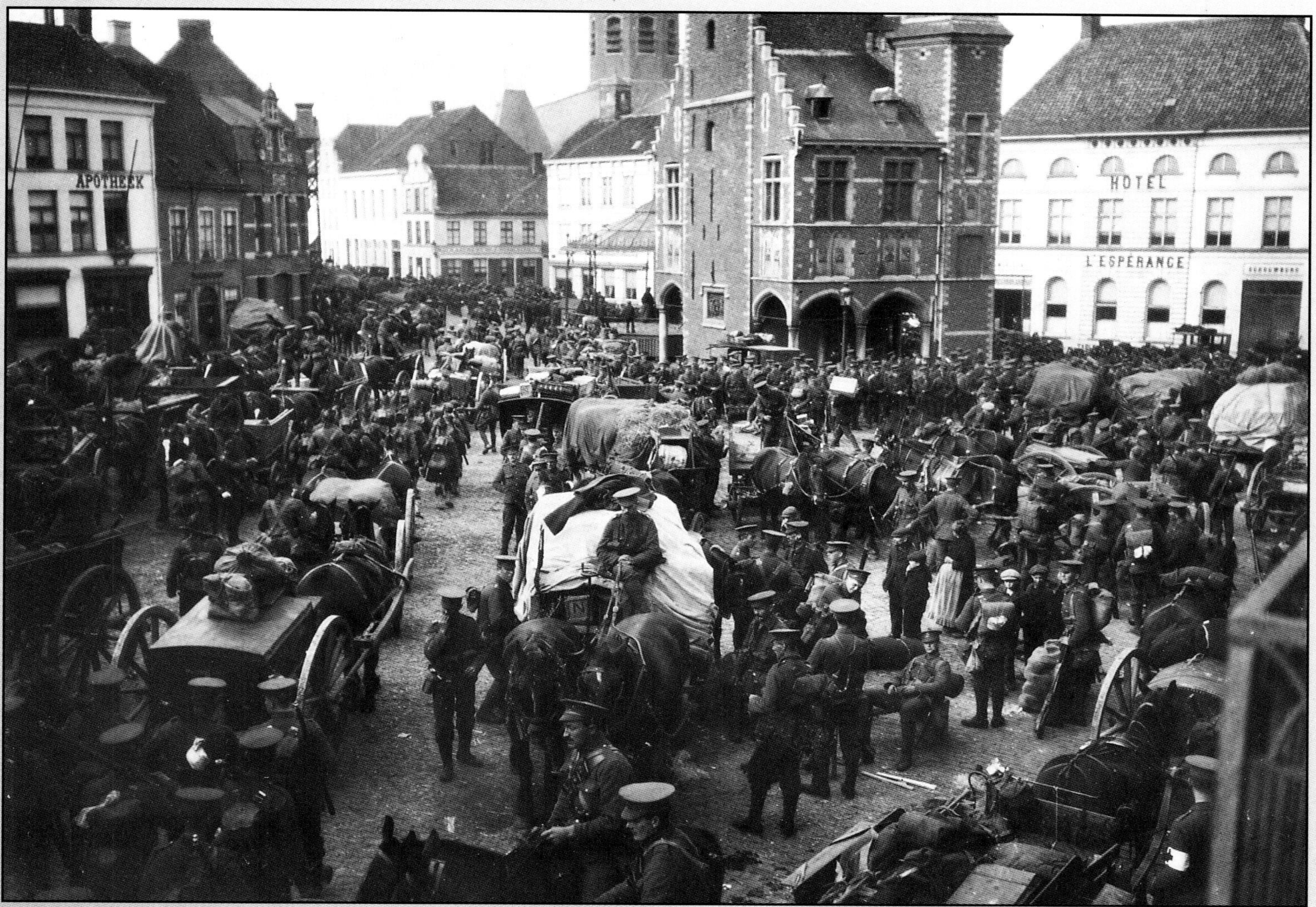
APOTHEEK
HOTEL
L'ESPÉRANCE

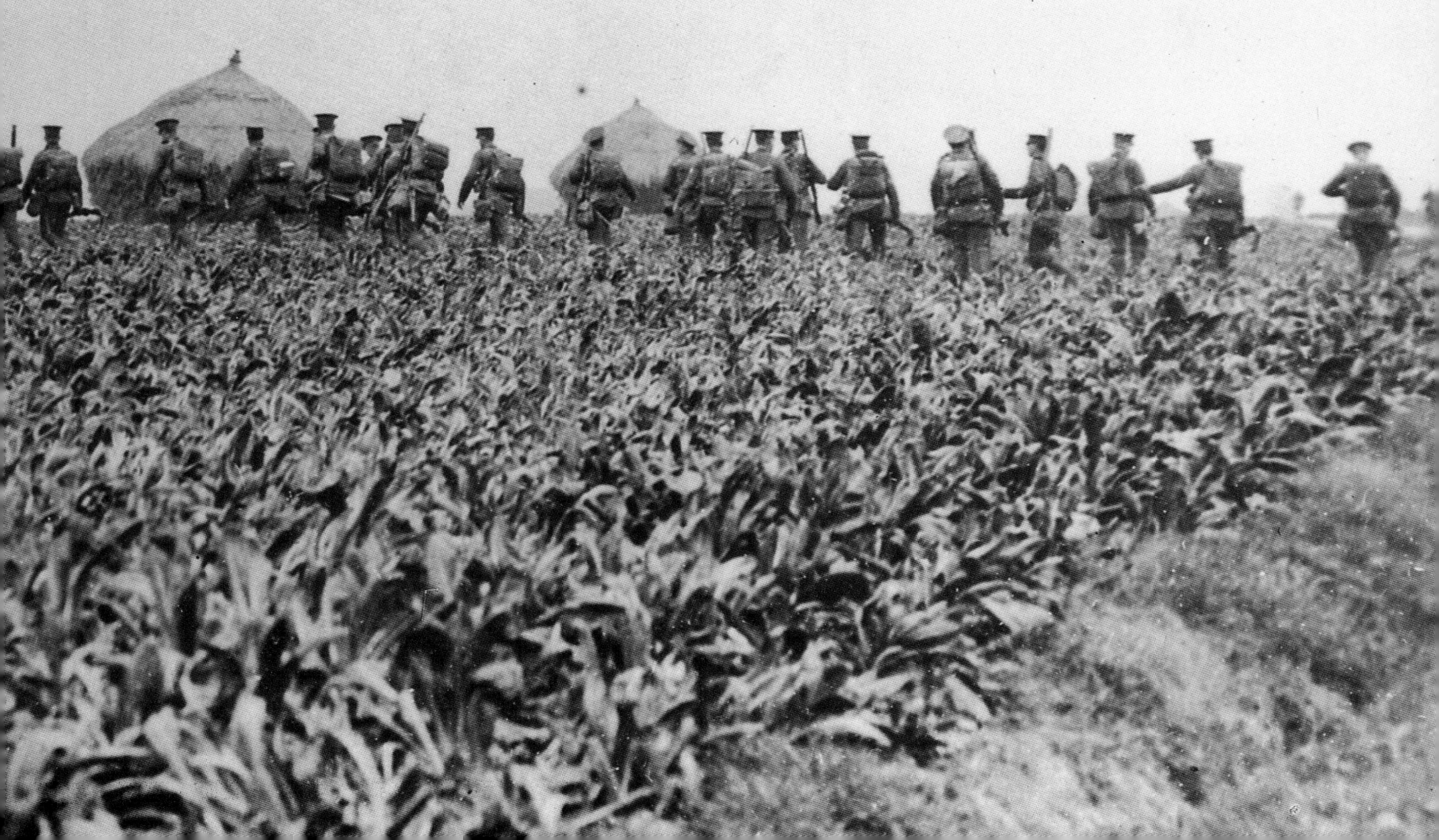

Left: The 2nd Scots Guards lead the reconnaissance in force towards Gheluvelt, 20 October 1914, during the First Battle of Ypres.

Right: Remnants of the London Scottish after the Battle of Messines, 31 October 1914. The ridge was captured by the Germans the following day.

Below right: Wounded Belgian troops from Furnes march through Calais, 11 November 1914.

Below, far right: French troops cycle to their positions near Wytschaete, October 1914.

Below: The First Battle of Ypres saw losses on both sides, the German failure to knock out the French ensuring a two-front war. 129th Baluchis march to the trenches near Hollebeke Chateau, 28 October 1914.

Top left: The 117,000-strong Belgian Army was both poorly trained and equipped in comparison with the other combatant nations. A Belgian machine gun section, its carts drawn by dogs, is pictured on the Western Front, December 1914.

Far bottom left: Waist-deep mud, water, lice and rats were among the hazards presented by trench warfare – and the horrors of gas were soon to come. 'C' Company, 1st Cameronians, are pictured in the trenches at Houplines, near Ypres in December 1914.

Above: French prisoners on the march under German escort, St Mihiel, 8 December 1914.

Below: British and German soldiers fraternise at Ploegsteert, Belgium on Christmas Day, 1914. The apparently spontaneous Christmas truce saw the combatants play soccer, exchange gifts and sing patriotic songs together – much to the discomfiture of the High Command of both sides.

Bottom left: British artillerymen prepare to fire in the Armentières Sector, 7 December 1914.

Top left: The German armored cruiser *Scharnhorst*, a key player in the balance of sea power in the Pacific as part of Vice-Admiral von Spee's East Asiatic Squadron.

Right: Rear Admiral Sir Christopher Cradock, killed at Cape Coronel off the coast of South America by von Spee's forces.

Bottom left: The British battleship *Canopus*, pictured at Mudros. *Canopus*, an old pre-dreadnought, was part of Cradock's squadron but he had left her behind when he encountered Spee at Coronel because of her slow speed.

Bottom: The German cruiser *Dresden*, one of Spee's squadron, is sunk off Juan Fernandez, 14 March 1915.

Top left: Although the *Dresden* escaped fatal damage at the Falklands, it was caught at Juan Fernandez where it is pictured flying the white flag of surrender.

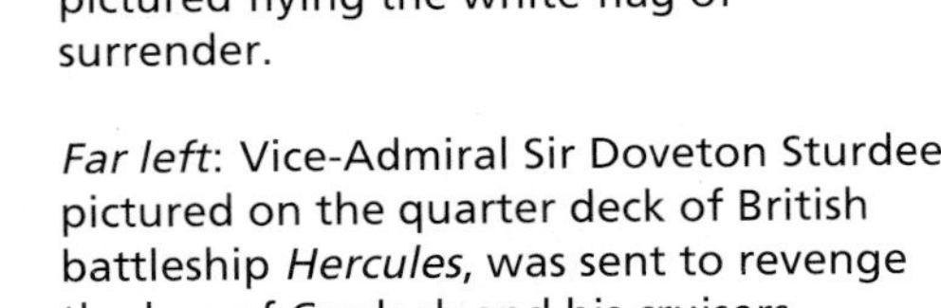

Far left: Vice-Admiral Sir Doveton Sturdee, pictured on the quarter deck of British battleship *Hercules*, was sent to revenge the loss of Cradock and his cruisers.

Left: Admiral Graf von Spee, who died along with his two sons and 2000 German sailors after a long-running battle with Sturdee's superior forces.

Below: The British Squadron (HMS *Kent, Inflexible, Glasgow*) seen from the maintop of a fourth ship, HMS *Invincible*, as they get under way from Port Stanley en route for the Battle of the Falkland Islands, 8 December 1914.

Top right: The German fleet pictured off the Chilean coast, November 1914. SMS *Scharnhorst, Gneisenau, Leipzig* and *Nurnberg* were all sunk at the Falkland Islands battle, 8 December 1914.

Bottom right: The aftermath of the Falklands battle: boats from HMS *Inflexible* pick up German survivors from the sunken *Gneisenau*.

Top left: A German naval landing party from the *Emden* prepares to leave Cocos Island, the alarm having been given from the *Emden*, 10 November 1914.

Bottom left: The German light cruiser *Emden* on the rocks after the engagement with HMAS *Sydney*, November 1914.

Above: The raiding activities of the German light cruiser *Emden* under Captain Karl von Müller in the Indian Ocean had attracted much attention from the Allies.

Right: Radio interception was critical in bringing the activities of the *Emden* to an end.

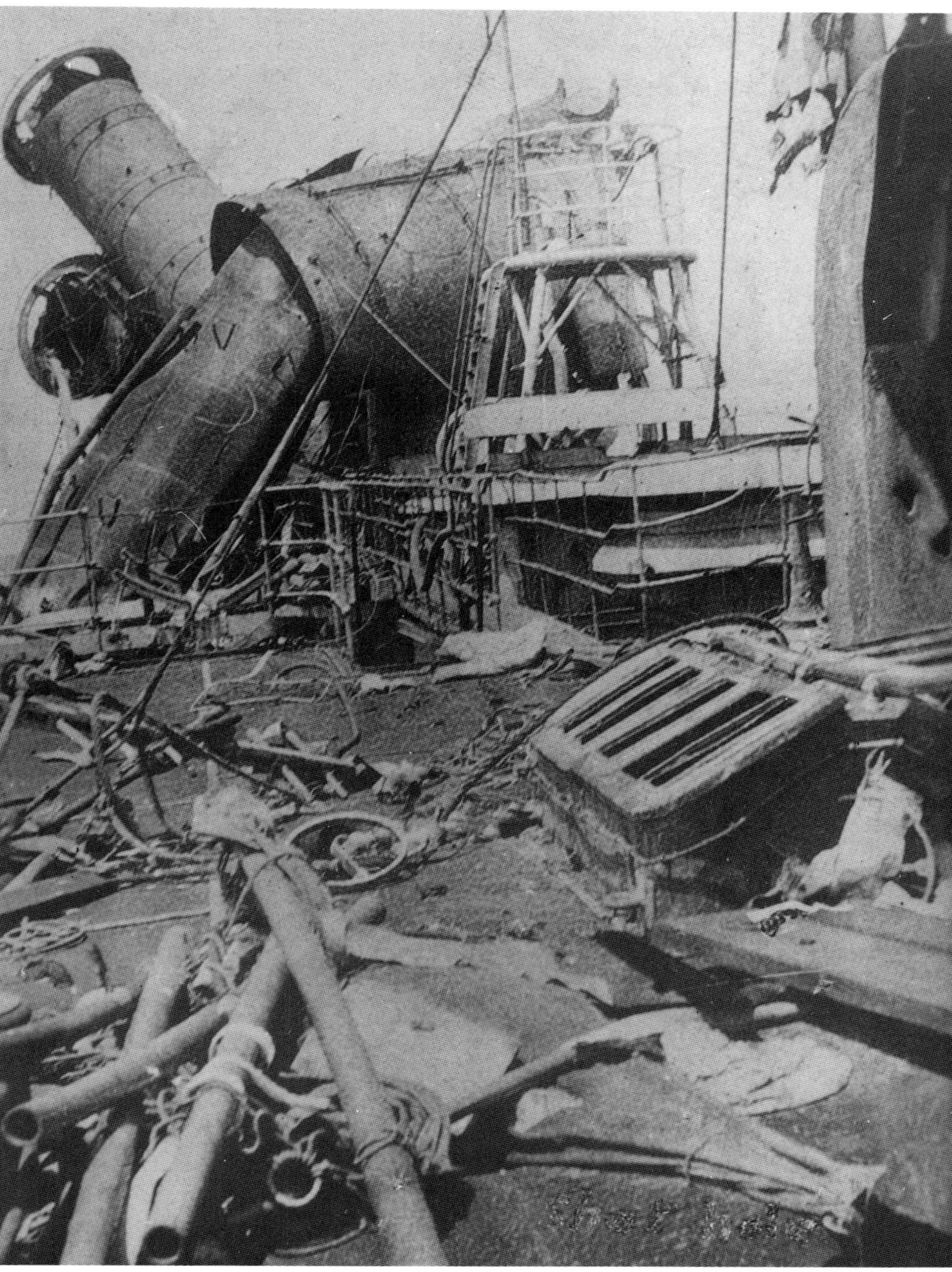

1915

The year opened with the first aerial bombing raid on Great Britain, carried out by a Zeppelin airship on 19 January. As would be expected, this and subsequent missions were intended to damage morale more than inflict tactical or strategic damage to military or civilian targets. Zeppelins dropped 6000 tonnes of bombs on Britain, killing 522 people, until a fleet of 11 was lost in October 1917 on a single raid – 10 to weather and one to home defenses. In June 1915 Flight Sub Lieutenant Warneford of the Royal Naval Air Service brought down a Zeppelin over Belgium. Though forced to land in enemy territory due to the severity of the explosion, he was able to regain his lines and was duly honored for the publicity-worthy feat.

In France, scout pilot Roland Garros and designer Raymond Saulnier combined to fit deflector plates on to the propeller blades of Garros's aircraft to permit bullets to be fired through the propeller arc: any bullets hitting the blades would be deflected safely clear. When Garros was shot down in April, the Germans inspected the machine but improved the concept, inventing the interrupter gear which linked the prop with the machine gun to ensure the weapon ceased firing in the instant it was obstructed. This was to have a revolutionary effect on combat above the Western Front.

If aviation warfare was in its infancy, so the nascent undersea threat was to come to the fore in no small way when February saw Germany mount the first submarine campaign in the seas around Britain. Even though fewer than 100 U-Boats were ever deployed at any one time and their building was deferred due to the concentration on capital ship construction, the U-Boat proved a surprisingly effective weapon of war: over 1,328,000 tonnes of Allied shipping were claimed over the year. The sinking of the liner *Lusitania* by a German U-boat on 7 May was the submarine's most spectacular single feat of the conflict. Though only 159 of the 1198 passengers lost were American, it was the first event extensively to influence public opinion in that still-neutral country.

On the Western Front, the French attacked the Germans in the Champagne area, but after promising initial advances were made with the aid of accurate artillery fire, the movement broke down into all-too-familiar trench warfare, both sides sustaining heavy casualties. British assistance was unavailing due to a shortage of guns and ammunition – a charge which, when relayed back home, helped bring down the Liberal government.

Turkey had signed a treaty with Germany quite unknown to the Allies and in October 1914 had started attacking Russian ports on the Black Sea. A clash on 1 January 1915 that left the Turks with only 18,000 survivors from a force of 95,000 led them to turn their attention to the Suez Canal.

The British had meanwhile determined to secure a route to Russia via Constantinople and the Bosporus. The task facing the mighty Royal Navy on the face of it seemed far from difficult – destroying Turkish forts before forcing entry to the Black Sea via the narrow straits connecting it with the Aegean. These were the Dardanelles, and Gallipoli was the finger-like peninsula guarding it. On 18 March, the first British attempt to force through the straits was made by a large fleet including 18 battleships. Three of these were sunk, while minesweepers in the lead were the first to turn

tail. A land offensive was the selected belated alternative, and on 25 April the Allies made a landing at Gallipoli.

The action was doomed from the start. It had been organised in haste, and the advantages were all with the defenders, the landing beaches being overlooked by rocky escarpments. Gallipoli was a frighteningly severe baptism of fire for the Anzacs, Australian and New Zealand troops who, with the British and Indians, made up the Allied assault force. The Anzacs (Australian and New Zealand Army Corps) had yet to be blooded but, volunteers to a man, they fought with extraordinary heroism against overwhelming odds: at one point they even hurled Turkish grenades back at the Turks. 16 Victoria Crosses were won in a single battle.

On 16 August a second series of initially more successful landings was made at Suvla Bay, but poor generalship and the inexperienced reserve troops the Allies employed allowed the Turks to regain the advantage.

After seven months of trench warfare that exceeded even the Western Front in its savagery, and cost some 200,000 men, the decision was made to withdraw. Achieved without the loss of a single life, that withdrawal – from 19 December to 9 January 1916 – was the most successful aspect of what had been a disastrous campaign in Allied terms.

With the Germans tied up on the Western Front, the Russians under Grand Duke Nicholas attempted to force their way on to the Hungarian Plain by attacking the Austrians at the Carpathians. The German counter to this with troops transferred from the stalemate in the West achieved spectacular results, advancing 100 miles in the Gorlice-Tarnow sector in just two weeks and capturing Warsaw on 4 August. The Russian army would ultimately regroup, but their morale was understandably at a low ebb.

Until early 1915 the British had played second fiddle to their French allies on the Western Front. Now after an initially successful blooding at Neuve Chapelle the BEF was divided into two armies, the First under Haig and the Second under Smith-Dorrien: the latter was involved with two French divisions at the 2nd Battle of Ypres in April, where the Germans used poison gas for the first time. Loosed at 5.30pm on 22 April, the chlorine gas initially caused panic and confusion in the Allied ranks, but with the advent of effective respirators was ultimately less life-threatening than irritating.

Italy joined the Allies on 23 May, believing they could deliver her the Italian-speaking areas occupied by Austria, her one-time ally, and notably the port of Trieste. Initial Italian attacks along the River Isonzo achieved little except heavy losses, however.

On the Western Front: Allied attacks at Artois, Champagne and Loos on 25 September failed. Britain was by this time deploying her Kitchener Army of still inexperienced volunteers, and losses sustained in trench fighting amounted to nearly 50,000.

The French deployed no fewer than 35 divisions in the Champagne offensive but failed to break through the German lines, a failure that underlined the fact that it was difficult to make gains in trench warfare, trenches being proof against anything but a direct artillery hit. Improvements in techniques such as sound ranging and flash spotting and the new tool of aerial reconnaissance improved the gunners' hand, but the stalemate on the battleground perisisted.

Previous page: A British 60-pounder battery in action at Cape Helles during the Gallipoli campaign.

Left: The twin 13.5-inch turret on the quarterdeck of the British battlecruiser *Queen Mary*.

Right: One of the early attempts to fit a forward-firing machine gun on a fighting aircraft. This Morane is fitted with a deflecter to knock aside bullets which would otherwise shatter the propeller. This makeshift device was soon overtaken by the interrupter equipment.

Left: Czar Nicholas II and Russian Commander-in-Chief Grand Duke Nicholas examine a report on the progress of the war.

Right: German forces claim yet another European capital as their cavalry enter Warsaw, 5 August 1915.

Below: Captured Russians pictured at Oporzec during the battles in Galicia on the Eastern Front.

Left: A lone Russian soldier pays his respects to his fallen comrades.

Right: Captured Russian artillerymen bring in their own guns after the Battle of Przemysl. Having been taken during the previous year's Galician campaign, the town was recaptured by Austro-German forces, 3 June 1915.

Below: German transport crosses the Vistula in 1915. Germany conquered Poland in that year and subsequently invaded Russia itself, capturing a million prisoners in 1916 alone.

Far left: General Hoffman, Chief of Operations on the staff of Hindenburg and Ludendorff. He used the experience gained as an observer with the Japanese Army against Russia in 1904 to good effect in 1914 and 1915.

Left: Major General Ludendorff, Chief-of-Staff to General Hindenburg.

Right: The appointment of 68-year-old Colonel General Paul von Hindenburg, replacing General Max von Prittwitz as head of the Eighth Army guarding East Prussia, was a surprise move in 1914.

Below: Russians prepare a counter-attack at Lemberg (Lvov), the Austro-Hungarian Empire's fourth city which eventually fell to them.

Left: Anzac Cove, Gallipoli. The Allied landings at the entrance to the Dardanelles met with massive resistance from the Turkish defenders, aided by the natural advantages of the rocky terrain: so many died that the sea was red with blood.

Right: King George V inspects the British 29th Division at Dunchurch, near Lymington, in March 1915 prior to their departure for Gallipoli.

Below right: A lighter or barge (foreground) at Sedd-el-Bahr, April 1915, is filled with Allied dead and wounded early in what was to prove a futile and bloody campaign. Several Victoria Crosses were won in this famous incident as troops tried to land from the transport ship *River Clyde*. The outcrop of rocks is where Commander Unwin VC rowed to pick up the wounded.

Below: The French battleship *Bouvet* sinks after striking a mine in the Dardanelles, 18 March 1915. The loss of the *Bouvet* was the first in a series on a day that ended with the abandonment of the purely naval attack to force the Dardanelles.

AB

Left: The Allied landing at Anzac Cove, 25 April 1915, the very first day of the Gallipoli campaign. Little headway was made against fierce Turkish resistance.

Right: In the face of weapons shortages the Allies improvised, making bombs (as grenades were then commonly known) from empty jam tins filled with old nails, bits of shell and barbed wire and other scraps of metal, and an explosive charge. A fuse was fitted through the top of the tin, to be lit with a match.

Below: A French 75mm gun in action near Sedd-el-Bahr during the third battle of Krithia, 4 June 1915.

Above: Four Commanders-in-Chief: Vice-Admiral A Boue de Lapeyrere (French Navy, C-in-C Mediterranean), General Sir Ian Hamilton, Vice-Admiral (Act) John M de Robeck, General Bailloud, GOC Corps Expeditionaire d'Orient. Hamilton was the British Commander-in-Chief at Gallipoli, but his lack of drive contributed greatly to the failure of the expedition.

Far right: Vice-Admiral Sir John de Robeck, KCB. De Robeck commanded the fleet which attempted to force the Dardanelles in March but withdrew after several ships were lost to mines.

Center: HMS *Ocean* was one of the old battleships sunk on 18 March.

Far left: The damaged periscope of the British submarine *E.11*, active in the Dardanelles against Turkish shipping.

Left: A trench scene at Anzac Cove, with men of the Royal Naval Division reinforcing the Australian and New Zealand Army Corps. The marines brought a few periscopes with them, and the Australians improvised a supply from looking-glasses sent ashore from transports.

Bottom left: The crew of HMS *Grampus* cheer submarine *E.11* as she comes out from the Dardanelles after sinking the old Turkish battleship *Barbarossa*. The *E.11* also had the unusual distinction for a submarine of claiming a train as one of its victims.

Right: Three French officers are pictured within the old fort at Sedd-el-Bahr, the guns having been destroyed by the British bombardment.

Below: A view of 'V' Beach at Gallipoli, taken from SS *River Clyde*.

Left: Sir Ian Hamilton leads the cheers for three officers of the French Mission whom he had just decorated. Next to him is General Braithwaite, his Chief-of-Staff.

Bottom left: Hay and petrol being placed among the boxes of stores in a dump at West Beach, Suvla Point, to be burned on evacuation, December 1915.

Right: Lord Kitchener returns with General Birdwood, walking through the trenches to Anzac Beach at Gallipoli, 13 November 1915. Kitchener agreed on his visit that the Gallipoli forces should be evacuated.

Below: Australian troops practise bomb throwing. Hand grenades, a weapon new to the Australians, were subsequently manufactured on the beach from jam tins and scraps of metal. These bombs were first issued in very small quantities about an hour before the third battle of Krithia, 4 June 1915.

Left: Australians make a bayonet charge at Anzac Cove, 17 December 1915. It was at Gallipoli that Australian and New Zealand troops, volunteers to a man, established their reputation as first-class fighting troops.

Below: An artist's impression of the Anzac landing brings home the hopeless task of defeating both the defending Turks and the inhospitable, rocky terrain that made high attacking casualties inevitable.

Left: The extensive damage evident in this picture, taken in Hartlepool in December 1915, was caused by shelling from German warships. The presence of the enemy within striking distance of the British homeland caused much public consternation.

Right: The spectacular demise of the German armored cruiser *Blucher* at the Battle of Dogger Bank, 24 January 1915.

Below: The *Blucher* pictured in happier circumstances before hostilities in 1910.

Right: The British battlecruiser *Indomitable* was sunk at the Battle of Jutland, the last great clash of massed 'battle' ships in history and the war's major naval battle.

Above: HMS *Taurus* shows off her sleek lines. The Royal Navy continued production of this basic type of destroyer from the 'L' class through to the 'R's until 1916, when demands from the Fleet led to a big jump in size and armament.

Left: The German battlecruiser *Derfflinger* was part of the German force at the Dogger Bank.

Below: The British battlecruisers *Lion* and *Tiger* also fought at the Dogger Bank where the *Lion* was Admiral Beatty's flagship and was badly damaged.

Above: The view from Kemmel Tower, near Ypres, in February 1915 shows the killing fields which were to claim so many young lives. At this stage the landscape is still comparatively unmarked by war.

Left: The 'Kitchener Blue' uniform as worn by the men on left and right compared with the standard uniform (middle), December 1914. Use of old blue uniforms was just one of the signs of shortages of equipment for Britain's new armies.

Above right: A colonel of the 1st Cameronians returns from his 'rounds' in a waterlogged trench at Bois Grenier, 5 January 1915.

Above far right: Men of the 11th Hussars warm themselves in front of a brazier in trenches near Zillebeke, February 1915. Cavalry units found themselves fighting side-by-side with infantry in the trenches as the progress of the war got bogged down.

Bottom right: A British motorcycle machine gun unit fires at enemy aeroplanes near Ypres, 1915.

BRITONS

"WANTS YOU"

JOIN YOUR COUNTRY'S ARMY!

GOD SAVE THE KING

Reproduced by permission of LONDON OPINION

Left: The much-copied poster by Albert Leete featuring the newly appointed Secretary of State for War, Lord Kitchener.

Below: The advent of gas, first deployed by the Germans at Ypres on 22 April 1915, led to the development of efficient gas masks. Improvised masks were used in the interim, as worn here by troops pictured in May.

Top right: Men of the Argyll and Sutherland Highlanders model Government-issue fur jackets in the Bois Grenier Sector, March 1915.

Bottom right: 'The Kensingtons at Laventie,' painted by Eric Kennington. The 'Kensingtons', or 1/13th Londons were a Territorial battalion in 56th Division.

Left: A French officers' mess in the field, August 1916.

Top right: An Indian machine gun team pictured near Querrieu, 29 July 1916.

Far top right: A battalion of the Scottish Rifles, on the march to take over positions from the French at Laventie, August 1915.

Right: A gas sentry sounds the alarm near Fleurbaix, June 1915. Initially devastating in its effect, the advent of efficient gas masks on both sides meant that by the end of the war gas was much less effective.

Far right: A French armored car equipped with an automatic anti-aircraft rifle takes up position near the front, 24 August 1915.

Below: 75mm French battery guns in action at Elberfeld, 1915.

Top left: The rate of attrition in the trenches meant those answering Kitchener's call soon found themselves in training – even when, like the pictured Sheffield City Battalion, their uniforms had yet to be delivered.

Left: Major Winston Churchill, wearing a French 'Adrian' shrapnel helmet, with General Fayolle, HQ, French XXXIII Corps at Camblain L'Abbe, 1915. Churchill resigned his office as First Lord of the Admiralty after the failure of the Dardanelles expedition (of which he had been an advocate) and served for a time in France.

Right: Some measure of conditions in which medical aid was rendered at the Front is given by 'Gassed and Wounded' by Eric H Kennington (1888-1960). Injuries deemed too serious to be dressed at the regimental first aid posts in the trenches were dealt with at a Casualty Clearing Station a few miles behind the front line.

Below: Lord Kitchener reviews troops of the New Army at Basingstoke, June 1915.

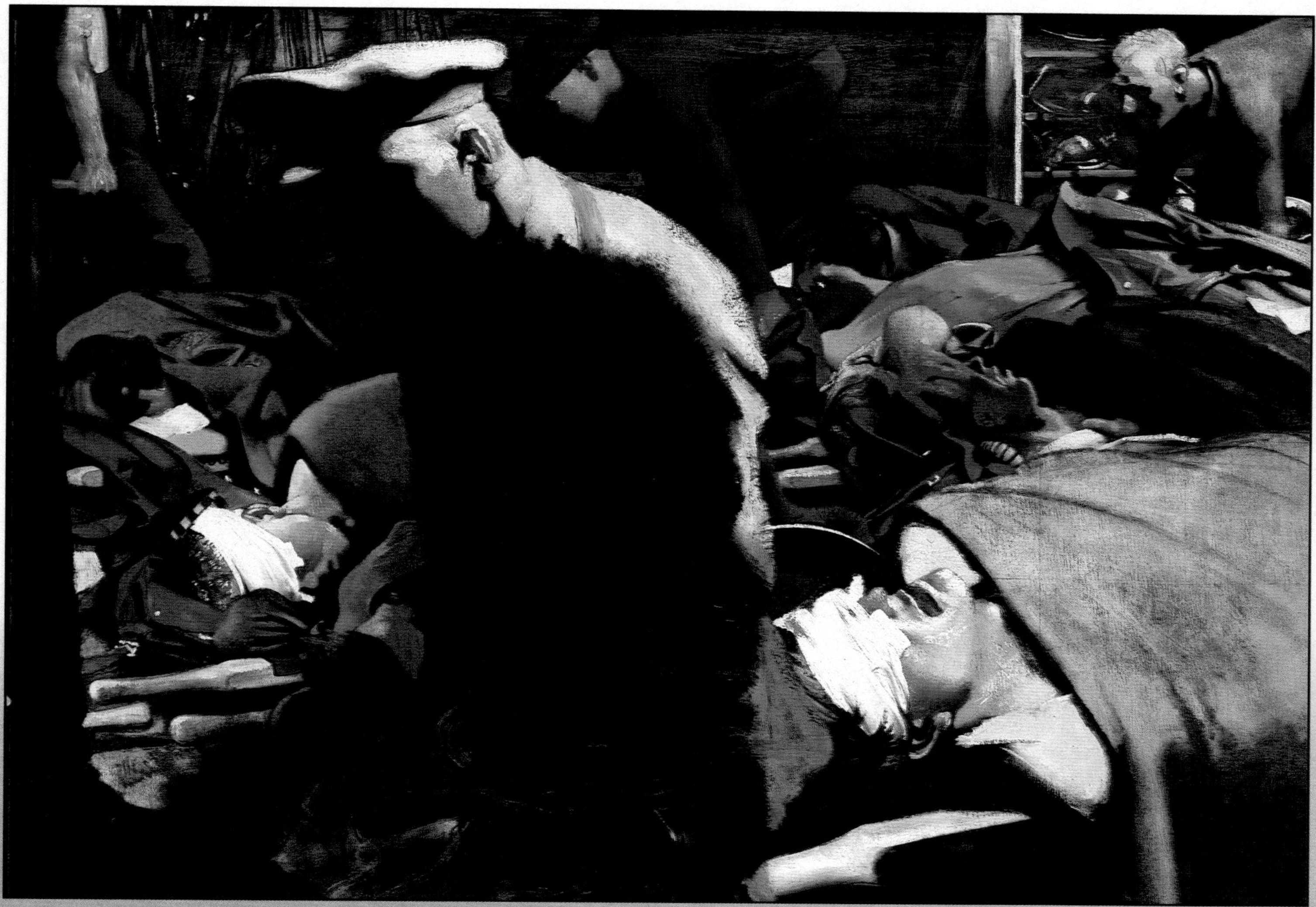

Left: An old French 155mm gun is dragged into action during the offensive in Artois, May 1915.

Above: Field Marshal Sir Douglas Haig (pictured) took over command of the BEF in 1915 and planned British battle strategy in France for the remainder of the war.

Top right: Compared with the British trenches, these French soldiers enjoyed favorable conditions in a front-line dug-out at Ravin de Souchez, October 1915. As the picture shows, the more colorful prewar French uniforms had by then been replaced by the more practical 'horizon blue'.

Right: A German Skoda-built 30.5cm howitzer is readied for action in the Argonne region, 1915.

Below: A French gun battery readies its 155mm weapons near Hassiges, Marne, September 1915.

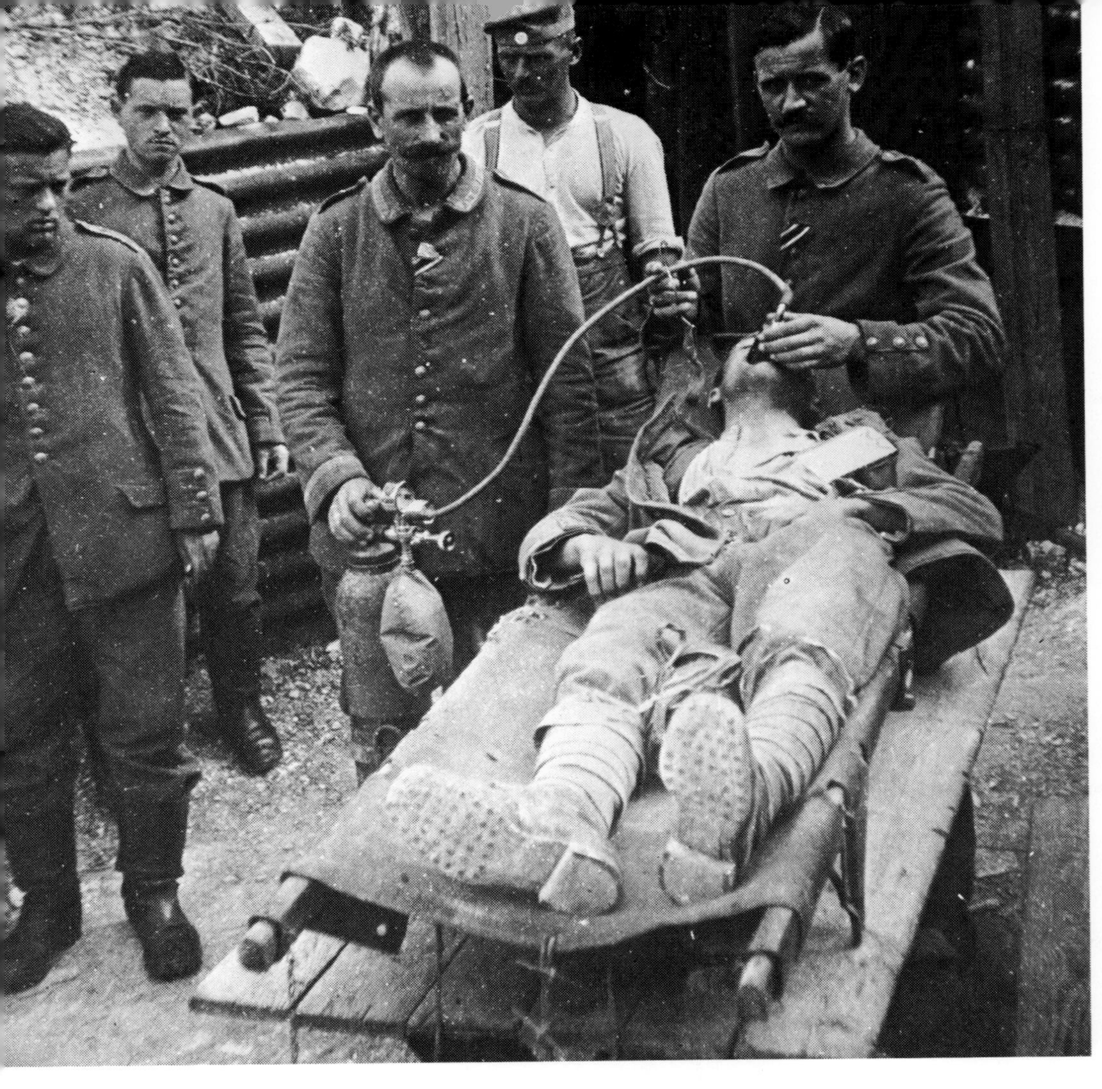

Left: Medical care in the German trenches – a gas casualty is treated. The introduction of gas in 1915 necessitated the development of new medical techniques to care for the wounded.

Below: German troops relaxing in a shallow dugout in a quiet sector.

Right: A French *poilu* with an improvised aerial torpedo. The French were quick to develop trench-warfare weapons, but many were unsuccessful.

Far right: Germans lay out pipelines before conducting a gas attack. Although gas shells were widely used as a delivery system, the older method was not entirely abandoned.

Bottom right: French artillerymen are pictured with their 220mm gun at Marne, October 1915.

Above: Men of the Scots Guards prime their Mills bombs in 'Big Willie' trench, October 1915.

Right: 'Come and buy your war bonds' reads the poster at the bottom of Nelson's Column in London's Trafalgar Square. The main attraction is to 'Bank at the tank', the revolutionary weapon of war displayed behind the crush barriers at center.

BANK AT THE TANK
OPEN HERE
MARCH 4th–9th
NATIONAL WAR BONDS
WAR SAVINGS
CERTIFICATES
COME AND
BUY YOUR
WAR BONDS
AT THE TANK
EXIT ONLY

272

Top left: The BE (British Experimental) 2a, a Royal Flying Corps mainstay in the early days of the air war, was more of a reconnaissance platform than a fighting machine, being renowned for its stability in flight.

Far left: This gun mounting evolved by Lt L A Strange was an early attempt to enable a gun to be fired by the pilot. The gun fired at an outward angle to clear the tips of the airscrew, so the pilot had to fly crabwise to aim and fire – unsurprisingly, it was not a great success.

Left: This Morane 'Bullet' features a deflector airscrew as developed in February 1915 by the French duo of pilot Raymond Garros and planemaker Raymond Saulnier. Not until Anthony Fokker's interrupter gear, however, did the fighter aircraft come of age.

Above: The Fokker EI of 1915 was unusual in having a monoplane configuration in a war where biplanes were the norm. The more powerful EIII with its interrupter gear was the mount of such aces as Max Immelmann, who claimed many slower Allied aircraft in the famous 'Fokker Scourge'.

Below: Aviatik B1 aircraft prepare German pilots for frontline service at the Aviatik Training School, Habsheim, 1915.

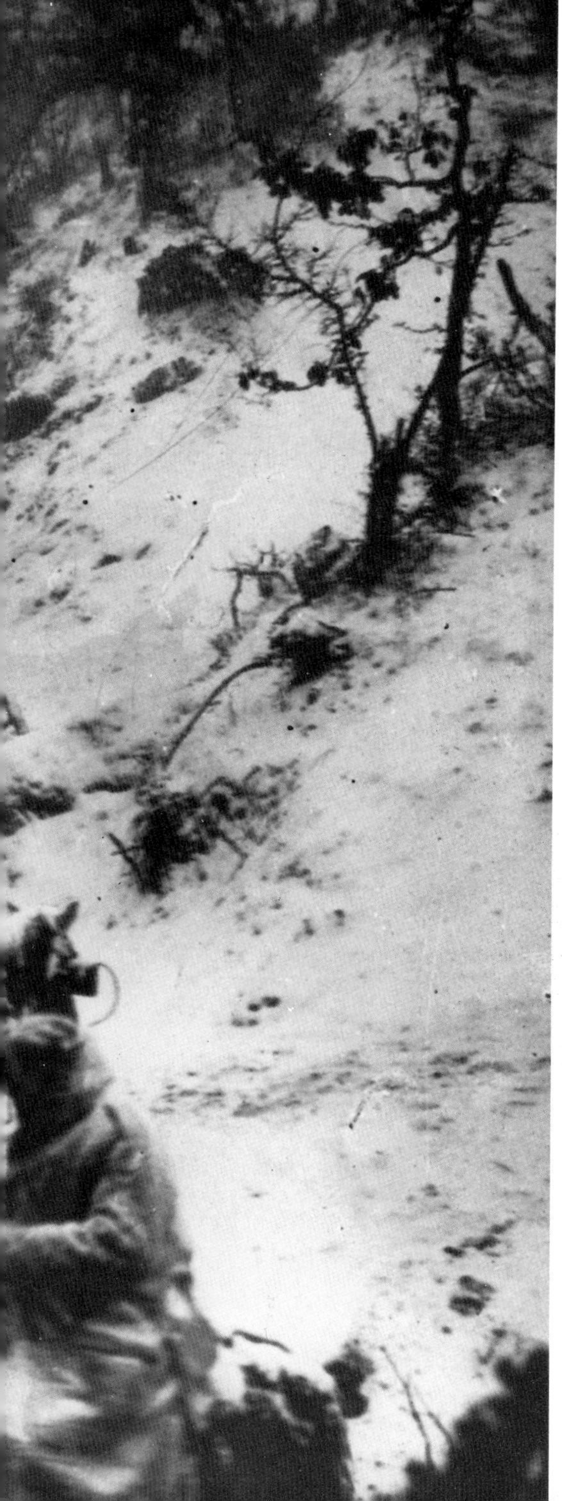

Top left: Serbian heavy batteries in action against the Austrians on the Macedonian Front. The refugee Serbs were re-equipped by the French after the Austrian occupation and were thenceforth valued allies.

Left: Serbian columns wend their way through inhospitable conditions during their terrible retreat.

Top right: Serbian cavalry at a river crossing. Serbs, Britons, Russians and Italians served side by side in Salonika – the mix of nationalities often leading to confusion.

Above: British troops wearing gas masks pictured in the trenches of the Salonika Front. The diversion of troops to the theater led German observers to dub it 'the greatest Allied internment camp' of the war.

Top left: Men of the Serbian 2nd Infantry Regiment pass through the town of Skopje en route to liberate their homeland from Austro-Hungarian occupation.

Bottom left: A column of Serbian howitzers at Krushivatz.

Right: A Serbian sentry pictured in neighboring Albania during the Salonika expedition.

Below: General Yankovitch of the Serbian Army.

1916

The year began with a US peace initiative brought to Europe by an envoy, Colonel House. But all attempts at mediation failed: both sides felt they had come too far to turn back, and by the following year 'hawks' would occupy all the relevant seats at the conference table.

The German attack on Verdun, an historic fortress town on France's eastern border, on 21 February was intended as the turning point in the war as they once more moved to the offensive in the West. For France, the loss of Verdun was unthinkable: it would be a great blow to morale, and the Germans believed they could inflict terrible damage on the French Army by attempting to take it. They brought men and artillery to Verdun in conditions of secrecy – completely outwitting the French, who had recently moved the fortress' heavy artillery to other sectors of the front.

Yet even though Verdun was surrounded on three sides and supplied by only one unprotected road, the Germans failed to take the town despite continuing to fight until the end of the year. At that point, nearly one and a half million men of both sides had fallen with little advantage gained by either. The dogged French resistance became something of a watchword, General Pétain achieving miracles in keeping the supply road open. The French turned to the offensive in July after the Somme had taken away German reinforcements and left them holding the upper hand. The Battle of Verdun finally ended on 15 December.

The face of naval warfare had changed when Britain launched HMS *Dreadnought* in 1906: by the outbreak of war, the Royal Navy had a fleet of 20 such vessels. With a speed of up to 25 knots and a displacement of 20-30,000 tonnes, these heavily armored ships could hit targets 30 kilometres distant with shells of 1000 or 1500 pounds. Simultaneously, however, the accuracy and destructive power of the torpedo delivered either from a submarine or surface torpedo boat rendered such vessels ever more vulnerable to attack. Dreadnought battleships of both sides, therefore, were rarely seen without a protective flotilla of destroyers and other vessels.

The greatest naval battle of the war, known to the British as the Battle of Jutland, took place on 31 May in the North Sea. Germany's High Seas Fleet, commanded by Admiral Scheer, hoped to catch an isolated portion of Jellicoe's Grand Fleet and thus whittle down the crushing British superiority in numbers. Instead the whole British fleet, forewarned by codebreaking of intercepted radio messages, was at sea. After initial engagements between the two sides' scouting forces of battlecruisers, the German fleet blundered into the British trap. Poor visibility and failures by junior British admirals to keep Jellicoe informed of German movements helped the Germans to escape before decisive damage had been done. During the following night the Germans successfully fled to their bases. Defective ship, shell and ammunition designs had meant that British losses were unnecessarily high and German damage comparatively low but, as an

Previous page: Devastation of months of battle on the Somme. The ruined building is the former church of the village of Beaumont Hamel, seen in November 1916.

Left: Both Britain and France made extensive use of troops recruited in their colonies for fighting in Europe and overseas. These are Annamese French Colonial Marine Infantry at Salonika in May 1916.

Right: By 1916 the artillery had clearly become the dominant arm in land warfare with a correspondingly massive appetite for shells. Here products of a British factory are being inspected.

American commentator pointed out at the time, the German fleet might have assaulted its gaoler but it had been firmly put back into prison once again.

One of the less glorious exploits of the British Army in the Middle East ended with the surrender of Major General Charles Townshend and his men at Kut on 29 April. Sent up the Tigris with Baghdad as its aim, Townshend's expedition ran into trouble at the end of 1915 and ended up beseiged in Kut where, despite aerial supply drops, the garrison raised the white flag seven months after taking the city. The result was a propaganda coup for the Turks.

Almost equally useless was the attack launched from Salonika against Bulgaria in December. Over 600,000 troops were fruitlessly employed there by the start of the following year: 'the greatest Allied internment camp' of the war, as one German cynic put it.

The British offensive on the River Somme, north of Verdun, commenced on 1 July. Originally intended for August, the attack was advanced a month to deflect the heat from the French at Verdun. Surprisingly for the British, a constant eight-day artillery barrage from one thousand guns failed to have any real effect on the Germans, who emerged from shelters dug up to 40 feet deep in the chalk soil to machine gun the advancing British at will. The first day of fighting saw casualties on a scale never before experienced in modern warfare, with 57,470 British casualties (including 20,000 fatalities)

The fighting lasted until November – and, as at Verdun, neither side could claim any advantage for an overall loss of nearly one million men. 142 days of fighting had brought few gains and as the winter of 1916-17 drew on, it was the British who were improving in standards of training; the German army of pre-war days had breathed its last.

One rare landmark of a featureless battle was the first successful use of tanks by the Allies. Developed by Britain, the armored vehicle in its Mark I form was relatively crude, but while many broke down one succeeded in capturing a village on its own. The War Office recognised its potential and promptly ordered 1000 of the improved Mark IV variety – machines that would come into their own in 1918.

On the Eastern Front, the Russian Brusilov Offensive mounted over a 90-mile front in April had pushed Austro-Hungarian forces back an astonishing 60 miles. It forced withdrawal of German units from the Somme to counter the threat in the East and, less happily, persuaded Rumania to side with the Allies – an unfortunate decision since her encircled position and obsolete army made her fatally vulnerable to attack. By December 1916 German forces under Mackensen were in Bucharest. This led to Russian resources being further stretched and dissipated any advantage gained. This would be Russia's last effective year as a war power although ironically the Russian factories were finally redressing the appalling armament shortages that had existed at the start of the war.

Above: Infantry of the 1st Canadian Division in the trenches at Ploegsteert, 20 March 1916.

Left: Grenade at the ready, a German sentry uses a periscope to survey No Man's Land in the Ypres area, 1916.

Top right: Men of the Northumberland Fusiliers enjoy a moment's light relief by wearing German helmets and gas masks captured at St Eloi, 27 March 1916.

Bottom right: Canadian infantry advance through Ploegsteert Wood, March 1916.

Top left: A sergeant major calls the roll shortly before his unit goes into action on the first day of the Battle of the Somme, 1st July 1916. No modern army suffered so many casualties in such a short space of time as did the British that day.

Far bottom left: Men of the 2nd Australian Division attend to Sunday lunch as best they can in a front-line trench at Croix du Bac, near Armentières, 18 May 1916.

Bottom left: Delousing, one of several grim but necessary routines that went hand-in-hand with trench warfare.

Above: The 18th Indian Lancers on the march to the front line, July 1916. Substantial cavalry reserves were assembled in the hope of a decisive breakthrough on the Somme.

Below: Australian troops in a front-line trench at Croix du Bac, near Armentières, use a makeshift mirror periscope to survey the action, 18 May 1916.

Left: The King of Montenegro and Commander-in-Chief of the British Expeditionary Force General Sir Douglas Haig, pictured at Beauquesne, south of Doullens, November 1916.

Below: An official Anzac photographer takes a picture of a barrage.

Top right: British Prime Minister Herbert Asquith (center, in hat) watches men adjust shell fuses outside Contay, 7 August 1916. He was succeeded by Lloyd George in December when public opinion demanded a change after the losses of Verdun and the Somme.

Bottom right: Logs are transferred to a light railway by British soldiers at a sawmill three miles west of Querrieu on the Amiens-Albert Road, November 1916.

Top left: Men of the 10th Australian Light Horse leave the defensive line on the Suez Canal, 10 June 1916, to destroy supplies of water in the Wadi um Muksahib.

Bottom left: Indian members of the Kut Expedition evidently suffering from severe malnutrition, photographed immediately after an exchange of prisoners with the Turks.

Right: Major General Charles Townshend's message to all ships and stations relating to the fall of Kut, dated 29 April 1916. The episode was Britain's greatest military disaster of the conflict and did much to further the Turkish cause in the Middle East at the expense of the British.

Below: General Townshend, whose poorly led and planned advance up the Tigris ended at Ctesiphon with retreat to (and an eventual surrender at) Kut-al-Amara.

Bottom right: Turkish troops take advantage of an unusual shelter from the heat.

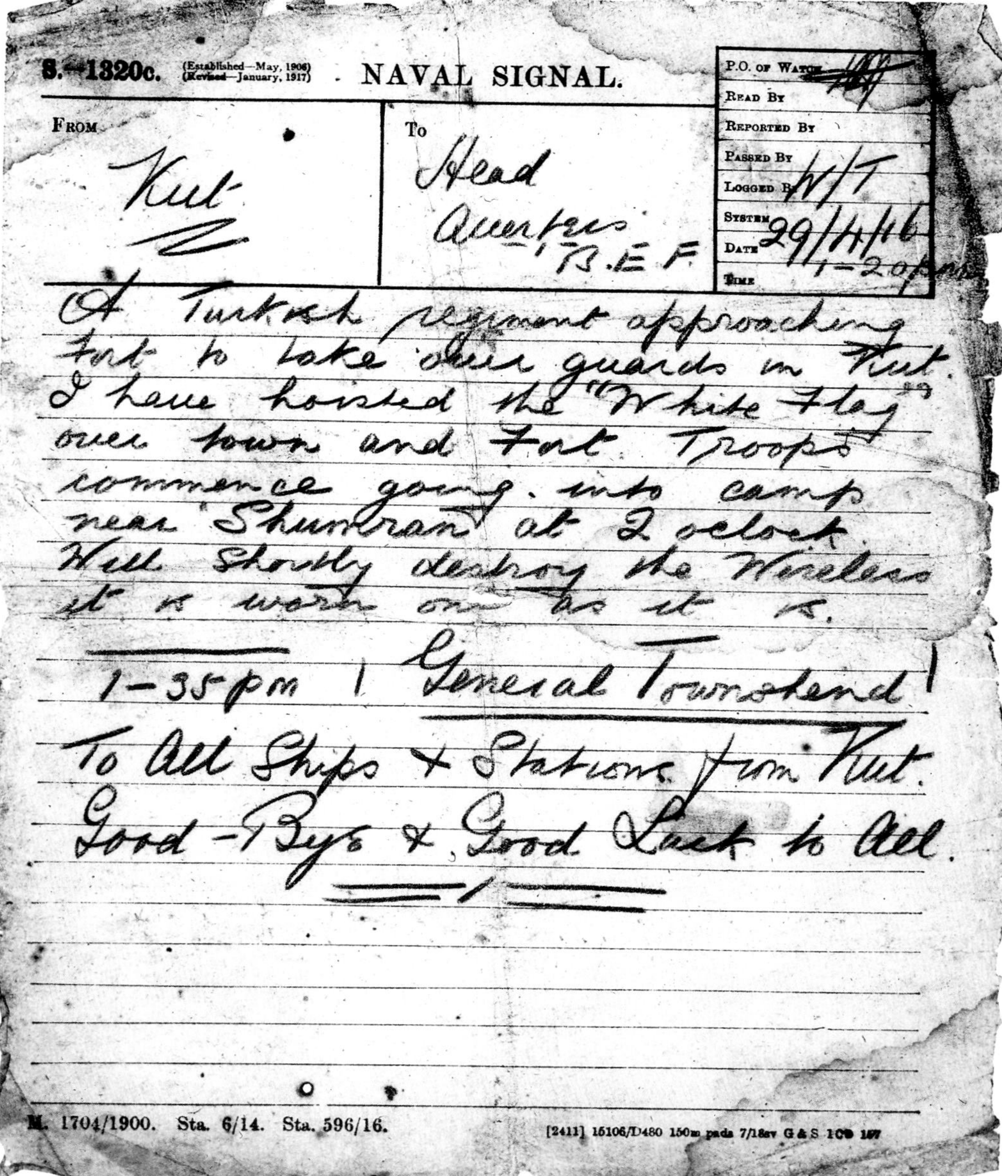

S.—1320c. (Established—May, 1906) (Revised—January, 1917) NAVAL SIGNAL.

P.O. of Watch
Read By
Reported By
Passed By
Logged By W/T
System
Date 29/4/16
Time 1-20 pm

From: Kut

To: Head Quarters, B.E.F.

A Turkish regiment approaching fort to take over guards in Kut. I have hoisted the "White Flag" over town and Fort. Troops commence going into camp near Shumran at 2 o'clock. Will shortly destroy the Wireless it is worn on as it is.

1-35 pm / General Townshend /

To All Ships & Stations from Kut. Good-Byes & Good Luck to All.

M. 1704/1900. Sta. 6/14. Sta. 596/16. [2411] 15106/D480 150m pads 7/18sv G & S 100 197

Below: French infantrymen turn a captured German machine gun against their enemy on the Mort-Homme ridge at Verdun.

Top right: French 155mm guns in action east of Roye.

Bottom right: Germans occupy a destroyed French artillery emplacement at Fort Vaux, Verdun, 1916. Falkenhayn rightly calculated that the French would accept any losses rather than give up Verdun. In the end, however, his own forces also lost very severely.

Far left: A French machine gun position in Fort Douaumont, scene of an early French reverse at Verdun. The weapon is a captured German Maxim.

Left: Oblivious to a French corpse close by, a German soldier takes aim from a trench at Verdun.

Above left: The French garrison of Fort Vaux, an exhausted medical orderly to the fore. Commandant Reynal surrendered on 7 June after an epic struggle when the water supplies finally ran out.

Above right: The German Crown Prince, surrounded by officers and soldiers, speaks to a medical orderly.

Below: Some of the many thousands of French POWs seized by the Germans at Verdun. The French held Verdun after a bitter ten-month struggle but at a cost of over 360,000 men.

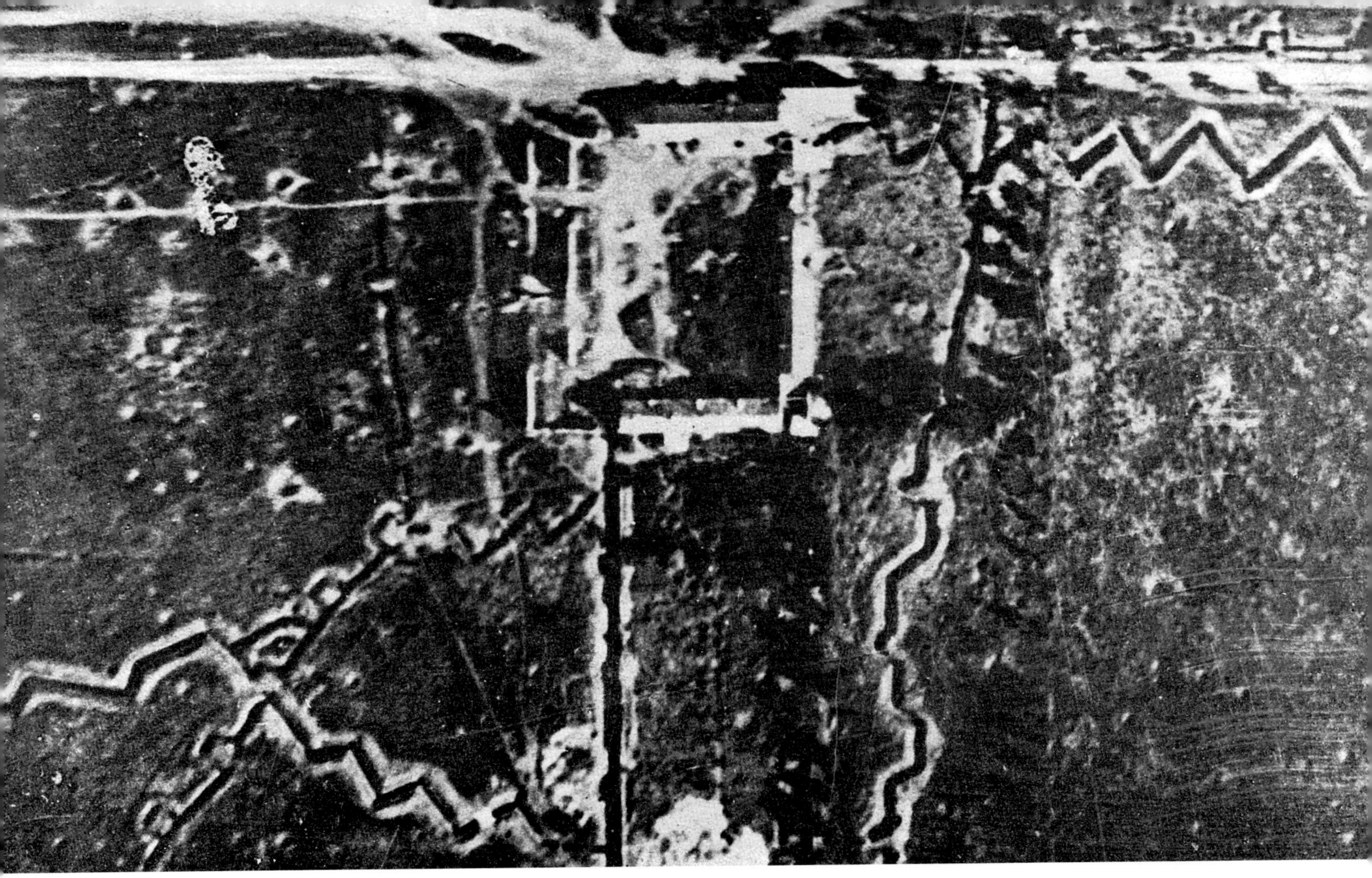

Left: This aerial photograph of Mouquet Farm shows both the extent of Allied trenches and the scars of enemy artillery shells.

Below left: French artillerymen on the Western Front.

Far bottom left: An artillery observation post near Vendresse on the Aisne.

Right: French troops prepare a mortar near Limey while awaiting a German attack, 5 March 1916.

Below: French wounded awaiting evacuation at Fort de Tavanne.

Top left: Defending a communication trench on the Oise with barbed wire.

Bottom left: Senegalese infantry on the march near St Raphael, Var, 18 June 1916.

Right: French gunners load a huge 400mm railway gun at Somme-sous-Marne, 4 April 1916.

Below right: The fiery, anti-German Georges Clemenceau, soon to be French Prime Minister, visits a French aviation camp near the front.

Far bottom right: General Joffre, Sir Douglas Haig and General Foch, pictured at Beauquesne, 12 August 1916. Though Joffre would lose his command of the French Army at the end of the year, Foch would eventually rise to command all Allied forces on the Western Front.

Below: A French 10th Army machine gunner with his pistol, bandoliers and equipment, pictured in the Somme area in August 1916

53
53

CLEMENCEAU VISITING FRENCH AVIATION CAMP NEAR FRONT.

Left: Jutland saw the British Grand Fleet (commanded by Admiral Sir John Jellicoe) and German High Seas Fleet (under Admiral Scheer) face to face for their only encounter of the war. The action of Admiral Scheer in withdrawing meant the British were unable to press home their advantage. The British battleship *Canada* is pictured.

Right: The German battlecruiser *Derfflinger*, one of the combatants at Jutland. She survived, but sustained damage.

Far right: Vice-Admiral Franz von Hipper commanded the German battlecruisers at Jutland and scored early success with the sinking of two British battlecruisers.

Below: German battleships on exercises, with the *Bayern* astern. The *Bayern* was the most powerful type of German battleship built for World War I but did not fight at Jutland.

Above: The German Nassau class battleship *Westfalen*, pictured in 1914. The *Nassau* was the first German dreadnought.

Left: Vice-Admiral Sir John de Robeck (right), a veteran of Gallipoli, pictured with Rear-Admiral Goodenough. Goodenough commanded a cruiser squadron at Jutland and was one of the few subordinates who served Jellicoe well with his scouting reports.

Top right: The sunken halves of HMS *Invincible*, the third battlecruiser to fall to German guns at Jutland, 1916. The destroyer *Badger* searches for survivors, observed by the photographer from the battleship HMS *Benbow*.

Below: The German battlecruiser *Seydlitz* limps home after being damaged at Jutland.

Top left: Destroyers of the 11th Flotilla escort battleships of the British Grand Fleet: HMS *Marmion, Marne, Prince Kempenfelt* and *Morning Star*.

Left: The British battlecruiser *Queen Mary* sinks off Jutland, 31 May 1916.

Top right: Safely back in port at Wilhelmshaven, the German battlecruiser *Derfflinger* shows damage incurred by shell fire at Jutland.

Above: The German pre-dreadnought battleship *Preussen*. The Germans were so outnumbered in modern ships that older pre-dreadnoughts still served with their main fleet.

Right: Rear-Admiral Horace Hood, lost with the sinking of HMS *Invincible* at Jutland.

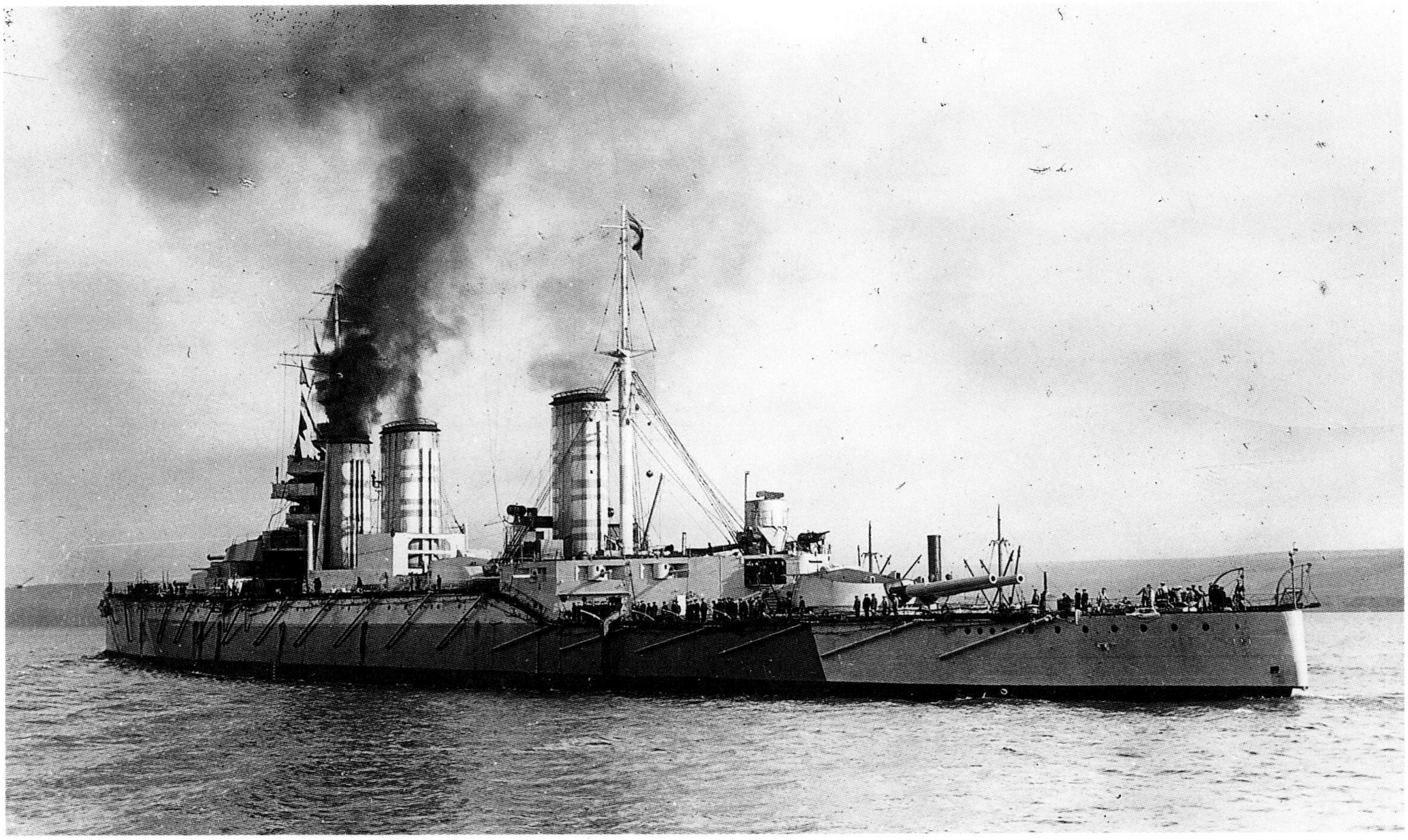

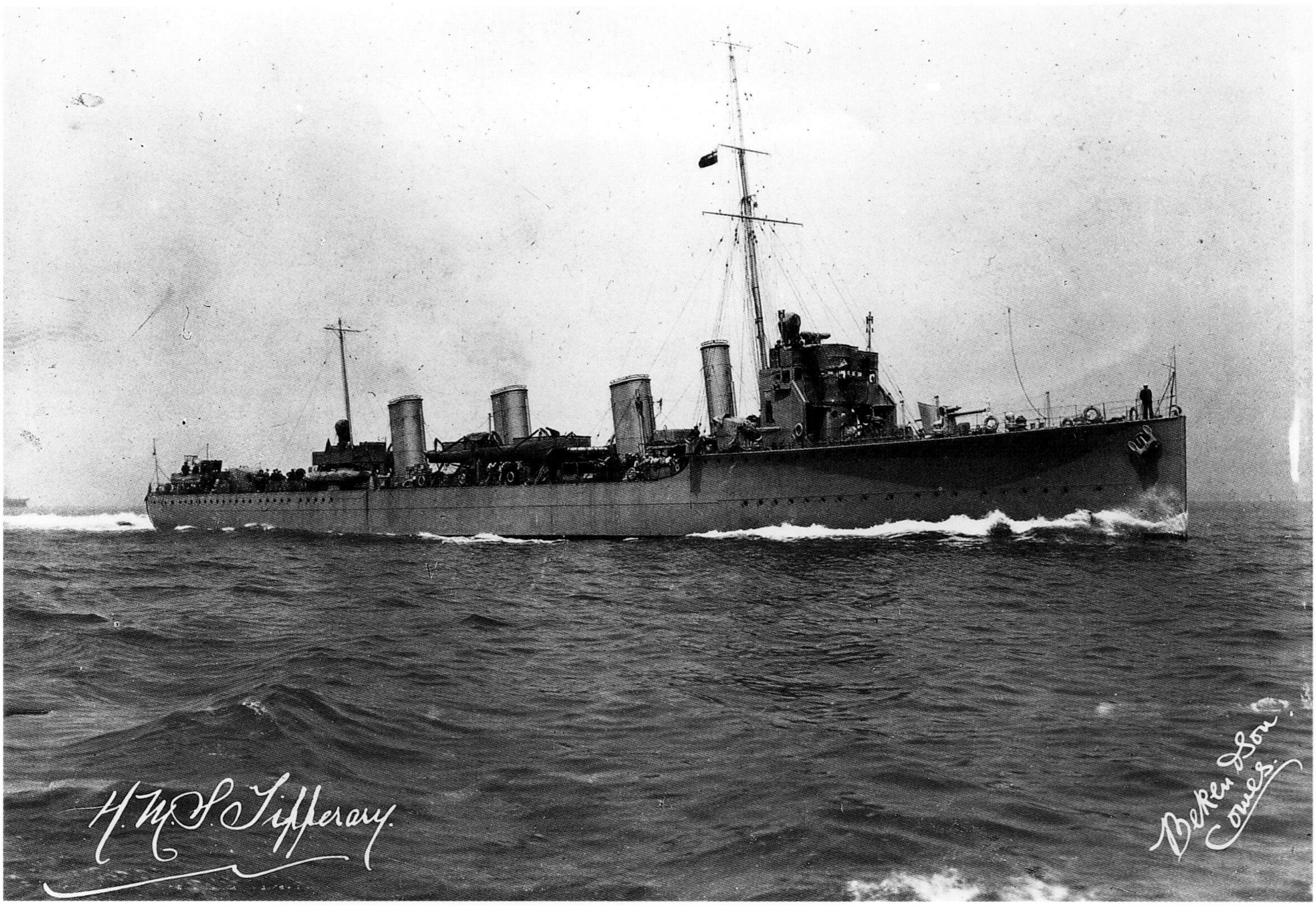
H.M.S. Tipperary.
Beken & Son, Cowes.

Top left: A British *Lion* class battlecruiser. The experience of Jutland would show that these ships were inadequately protected.

Bottom left: The British destroyer *Tipperary*, sunk at Jutland. The Royal Navy's casualties in the action, 6017, were nearly double those of the Germans, losing three battlecruisers and three armored cruisers as against one battlecruiser, a battleship and three armored cruisers.

Below: The German battlecruiser *Seydlitz*, in port and showing signs of the severe damage sustained during the Battle of Jutland. Admiral Sir John Jellicoe was blamed by many for letting the German Fleet slip back to port, but Churchill stoutly defended him.

Right: Vice-Admiral Sir Hugh Evan Thomas, Flag Officer commanding the Fifth Battle Squadron at Jutland, pictured with his dog Jack.

Bottom: With 14 guns in 7 twin turrets, the Royal Navy's *Agincourt* was one of the heaviest-armed ships at Jutland. *Agincourt* had originally been ordered for Brazil but had been bought by Turkey. Almost complete in 1914, she had been taken over by the Royal Navy. Although Britain paid for the ship, this 'insult' was one of the main causes of Turkey joining Germany in the war.

Left: Admiral Sir John Jellicoe, commander of the Grand Fleet, famously described as the 'only man who could lose the war in an afternoon.'

Above: British naval ratings enjoy a meal in one of the mess decks of a Royal Navy battleship.

Right: Prince Henry of Prussia (with field glasses) pictured with Admiral von Scheer, Commander-in-Chief of the German High Seas Fleet at Jutland. Although Scheer had fought the battle creditably, the German fleet was not to play further significant part in the war.

Bottom right: HMS *Black Prince* pictured prior to the outbreak of war in 1914. *Black Prince* was one of the armored cruisers sunk at Jutland.

Bottom left: The 1st Lancashire Fusiliers are addressed by their divisional commander, Major General de Lisle (on horseback), before the Battle of the Somme, 29 June 1916.

Bottom right: Smoke rises from the German trenches as a British artillery bombardment heralds the first day of the Battle of the Somme, 1 July 1916.

Below: British infantry of the 34th Division advance on La Boisselle, 1 July 1916. So bad was the carnage on this, the opening day of the Somme, that German officers permitted a temporary truce in some areas to remove the scores of badly wounded from the battlefield.

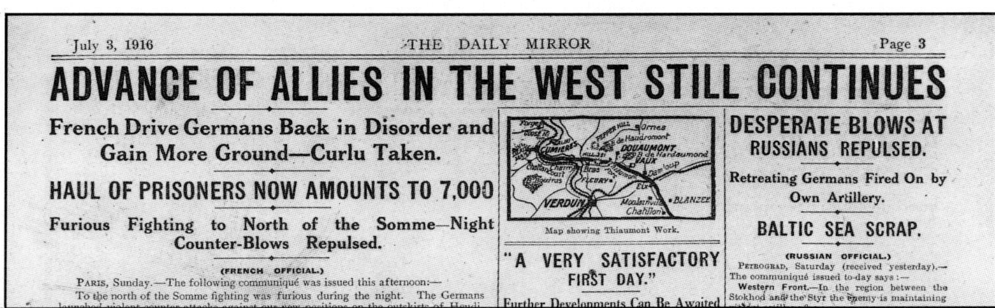

July 3, 1916 THE DAILY MIRROR Page 3

ADVANCE OF ALLIES IN THE WEST STILL CONTINUES

French Drive Germans Back in Disorder and Gain More Ground—Curlu Taken.

HAUL OF PRISONERS NOW AMOUNTS TO 7,000

Furious Fighting to North of the Somme—Night Counter-Blows Repulsed.

(FRENCH OFFICIAL.)

PARIS, Sunday.—The following communiqué was issued this afternoon:—

To the north of the Somme fighting was furious during the night. The Germans

Map showing Thiaumont Work.

"A VERY SATISFACTORY FIRST DAY."

Further Developments Can Be Awaited

DESPERATE BLOWS AT RUSSIANS REPULSED.

Retreating Germans Fired On by Own Artillery.

BALTIC SEA SCRAP.

(RUSSIAN OFFICIAL.)

PETROGRAD, Saturday (received yesterday).—The communiqué issued to-day says :—

Western Front.—In the region between the Stokhod and the Styr the enemy is maintaining

Left: British troops at the entrance of a captured German dug-out on the Somme, July 1916. Deep dugouts like this could survive all but a direct hit from the largest gun.

Above: The headline 'A very satisfactory first day' refers to the Battle of the Somme and is totally misleading: 1 July 1916 was in fact the worst day in British Army history with some 57,000 casualties sustained.

Right: A British 12-inch gun on railway mountings in action, August 1916.

Far right: Lieutenant-General Sir Henry Rawlinson, the man entrusted with the initial attack on the Somme, pictured outside Fourth Army Headquarters at Querrieu Chateau, July 1916. His preference for a slow, methodical advance proved less than successful in practice.

Below: British troops of the 31st Division march to the trenches, 28 June 1916. This platoon is from the 10th Battalion East Yorkshire Regiment, better known as the Hull Commercials, one of the 'Pals' Battalions.

Top left: An early design by Dutchman Anthony Fokker, the *Spin* monoplane, was a widely-used German trainer in the very early war years.

Left: The sturdy Junkers J1 ground attack aircraft, built entirely out of steel sheets, was first flown in December 1915 and rejoiced in the nickname of 'Blechsel' (Tin Donkey).

Above: Sgt R Soubiran of the Lafayette Escadrille, pictured at Cachy Aerodrome on the Somme during the 1916 offensive. The Escadrille housed a diverse group of American pilots who, after their country's entry into the war, became the 103rd Aero Squadron; Soubiran became its commanding officer.

Right: James McConnell, one of the Lafayette Escadrille's original nine pilots, pictured in 1917. The Marquis de Lafayette was a Frenchman who had fought for America during the War of Independence, hence the unofficial name of Escadrille N 124.

Below: A De Havilland DH-2 single-seater 'pusher' biplane takes off from Beauval Aerodrome. The pennant flying from a wing strut indicates a Flight Commander's machine. The advent of interrupter gear saw such machines quickly superseded by more maneuverable 'tractor' types, with propeller at the front.

Left: The interior of a German airship. Although Zeppelins were used to bomb Britain between 1915 and 1916, their raids were of nuisance value only and the development of efficient anti-aircraft defenses meant they were phased out in favor of Gotha and Giant fixed wing types.

Above: This aerial photograph of a German airship outside its hangar at Witmundshaven indicates the vast size of the Zeppelins.

Right: Air mechanics bring up a gas-filled 'nurse' balloon to fill a larger observation balloon near Meaulte, on the Bray-Albert Road, 7 August 1916.

Bottom right: The gondola and crew of a German airship.

Above: A German airship is caught or 'coned' in the network of spotlights installed around London in 1916. Anti-aircraft fire and night fighters would then be deployed against the dirigible.

Below: Wreckage of German Zeppelin airship *L.31* brought down at Potters Bar, 2 October 1916. The first Zeppelin killer, the Royal Navy's Flight Sub Lieutenant Warneford, received a Victoria Cross for his feat.

Above right: The gondola and other wreckage of Zeppelin *L.32* brought down by 2nd Lt F Sowerby of No 39 Home Defence Squadron RFC, flying a BE2c biplane on 23 September 1916. The German crew perished.

Top left: Oberleutnant Max Immelmann was killed in a dogfight on 18 June 1916 – but not before the Immelmann turn, a slow roll off the top of a loop, had entered the air combat vocabulary.

Top right: Raoul Lufbery, Escadrille Lafayette's highest-scoring ace, seated on his Nieuport while it is primed for take off.

Above: Werner Voss was considered by many to be the equal of the Red Baron von Richthofen himself. His death after single-handedly fighting seven RFC adversaries in September 1917, was mourned by the Allies as well as the Germans.

Right: Oswald Boelcke was one of the greatest tacticians in the early days of air fighting.

Left: British machine gunners, pictured with their gas helmets on, fire on a German communication trench near Ovillers during the opening days of the Battle of the Somme, July 1916. The initial attack was brought forward a month in an attempt to relieve the French, then in desperate straits at Verdun.

Below: Men of the Border Regiment rest in a front-line trench, Thiepval Wood, August 1916. German defenses at Thiepval were so strong that, despite having initially been a first-day objective, the British only succeeded in taking Thiepval Ridge at the end of October.

Left: A British Army officer observes the course of the Battle of Bazentin Ridge from the ruins of a church, July 1916.

Right: German walking wounded, captured early in battle by the British on the Somme, July 1916. Action at the Somme dragged on unresolved until November, taking a prodigious toll in the lives of both sides. German commanders, whose losses neared half a million, later admitted the Somme was 'the muddy grave of the German field army'.

Far right: General Sir William Robertson, depicted by artist Francis Dodd in 1918. Quartermaster-General of the British Expeditionary Force in 1914, Robertson was Chief of the Imperial General Staff from 1915-18.

Below: Horse-drawn British artillery limbers bring up ammunition during the Battle of Pozières Ridge, July 1916.

Top left: The British attack near Mametz, 1 July 1916. The white marks on the ground show where trench digging has exposed the underlying chalk in this area.

Bottom left: The British Mk 1 tank, an example of which is pictured at Chimpanzee Valley on the Somme in September 1916, during the first battle in which tanks were used. Many early models broke down – but one captured a village on its own, leading the War Office to order 1000 improved Mark IVs.

Above: Men of the 15th (Highland) Division march back from the front line to rest headed by their pipers after successfully taking Martinpuich during the Battle of Flers-Courcelette, 15 September 1916.

Below: King George V, General Sir Douglas Haig and commander of the Fourth Army General Sir Henry Rawlinson, pictured in August 1916.

Below: Stretcher bearers carry a wounded man over the top of a trench at considerable personal risk in the village of Thiepval during the hard-fought Battle of Thiepval Ridge, 26-28 September 1916.

Bottom right: Artist Colin V Gill's depiction of a battery of 9.2-inch howitzers. Their patchwork camouflage made them unrecognizable to hostile aircraft, while the green netting helped to conceal the emplacements. On the right of the picture are two infantrymen resting by the gun-pit on their way back from the front line, and on the left is a wayside calvary broken and overturned by a shell explosion. The Forward Observing Officer and his signal sergeant, leaving the battery for the observation post in the front trenches, and a ruined village in the background form part of the decorative scheme.

Left: Cavalrymen of the Queen's Bays approach Hardecourt Wood on the march during the Battle of Flers-Courcelette in September 1916, hoping in vain to exploit a breakthrough in the German lines.

Bottom left: Conditions in this trench near Trones Wood, November 1916, bear witness to the fact that the winter of 1916-17 was the worst in living memory. The British troops pictured here have a difficult – if not impossible – task on their hands cleaning it out.

Right: British troops receive rations from field kitchens in the Ancre area, October 1916. The availability of hot food was a much-needed morale booster in the cold, wet and inhospitable conditions of the Somme campaign.

Below: Ration wagons on the muddy road to Montauban, November 1916. The capture of that village by British forces on 1 July was the sole success of the bloody first day of fighting in the Somme.

Right: Heavy artillery played a decisive part in the conduct of the war on the Western Front. Guided by observers in the front line sending back direction and range instructions by field telephone, their power pinned down troop movements, causing a higher loss of life than any other weapon used in the war.

Below: The early morning scene before the British on Thiepval, 15 September 1916. The rockets and incendiary flares were used by front-line troops requesting their artillery to lay down a defensive wall of fire through which the enemy advanced at his peril.

Bottom: Men of the Gordon Highlanders pull on rubber thigh-boots in anticipation of wet and wintry conditions ahead, Bazentin-le-Petit, November 1916.

Above: Rumanian infantry in their parade uniform in Bucharest on their country's declaration of war against Austria-Hungary on 27 August 1916. This proved an ill-judged move, in view of her poor strategic position surrounded by enemies and the fact that her army was equipped with obsolete weaponry.

Left: General Alexei Brusilov, commander of the Russian Southwest Army Group, whose surprise, wide-fronted advance against Austria-Hungary on 4 June 1916 bore fruit in the north and south, taking 200,000 prisoners and liberating much enemy equipment en route.

Left: German soldiers pictured in Bucharest after that city's fall on 6 December 1916.

Below: A German 21cm howitzer is sited within its emplacement in preparation for an assault on Rumanian positions at Sereth.

Right: Russian troops await the order to attack in a trench near Tarnopol, July 1916. By September, they had successfully and speedily advanced westward some 40 miles further into Galicia in what was known as Brusilov's Offensive.

Far left: General August von Mackensen, German commander of the Austro-German-Bulgarian force that crushed Rumania.

Left: German cavalrymen armed with lances ride through a Russian village, January-February 1916.

Bottom left: Russian troops on the Balkan Front halt on the roadside, September 1916. Each man carries a French Adrian-pattern steel helmet.

Bottom right: An Austrian crew adjusts the sights of a 30.5cm howitzer at Simemakowce.

Right: General of Artillery Nikolai Ivanoff, commander of the Russian Southern Army Group that won a major victory over the Austrians in Galicia.

Генералъ-отъ-артиллеріи Н. І. ИВАНОВЪ, командующій войсками кіевскаго военнаго округа.

Left: British troops in the Balkans take their daily five-grain Quinine issue, July 1916. Such medication was compulsory and would always be taken under supervision to ensure men did not take the 'soft option' and allow themselves to fall sick.

Below: General Sarrail inspects the Russian troops upon their landing at Salonika, 30 July 1916.

Top right: The Serbian Army, newly equipped by the French, marches to camp at Mikra, April 1916.

Bottom right: The personnel of a French field kitchen with the Corps Expeditionaire d'Orient prepares food within half a mile of the Turkish line.

Top left: Italian troops of the 35th Infantry Division march through Salonika, August 1916.

Left: Russian troops move to a forward area, following their arrival in Salonika in September 1916.

Above: Artist Stanley Spencer's depiction of Allied casualties arriving by means of mountain ambulance transport at a dressing-station at Smol, Macedonia, September 1916.

Right: Serbian troops outside their shelters in a frontline trench at the Battle of Florina, September 1916.

Above: British officers of 27th Division pictured in an off duty moment playing badminton in the Greek village of Stavros, November 1916.

Below: Saxon Jäger troops in action near Monastir, December 1916.

Top right: A Serbian infantry battalion on the Balkan Front prepares to resume its march after a bivouac, December 1916.

Bottom right: A British 18-pounder in action, November 1916. The British forces at Salonika occupied the right of the Allied line, thereby facing a formidable foe in the Bulgarian Army.

Above: Austrian troops in a mountain pass in northern Italy.

Left: The Italian destroyer *Giuseppe Carlo Abba*, pictured leaving the port of Brindisi, September 1916.

Top right: Italian mountain troops were said to be among the most efficient in their army.

Bottom right: Austrian troops man a machine gun in the Alps.

Above: Public war cooking helped feed the German population. The Allied naval blockade gradually reduced food supplies in Germany despite a careful rationing system.

Left: The mobilisation of menfolk to fill the huge gaps in the Army ranks created by the Somme and other battles led to women taking over previously male-only jobs, as illustrated by this picture of a lady tram driver at Lowestoft in England.

Top right: The Countess of Rosslyn lends the British Red Cross her assistance at Boulogne, one of the forms of 'war work' more commonly taken up by ladies of higher social standing.

Bottom right: In the absence of horses, needed for the war effort, a team of dogs draws a harrow at this farm near Reninghelst, April 1916.

Top left: Shell making at Hadfield's Works at Sheffield. An early scarcity of ammunition for the British led to the formation of a Ministry of Munitions, but the quantity and quality available to the Allies increased dramatically as the war progressed.

Left: British problems extended further than the Western Front. A Sinn Fein prisoner is escorted to Dublin Castle after the Easter Rising in Ireland in 1916.

Above: A view of the howitzer shop in the Coventry Ordnance Works. Heavy caliber artillery was at a premium in the early days of the war.

Right: Women were also proving increasingly crucial to the German war effort; the predominantly female workforce of an armament factory is pictured.

OLD HUN
LINE.

1917

On 1 February, the Germans declared unrestricted U-Boat warfare against Britain and France. At the height of their success in early 1917 they accounted for 470 ships in three months while the top-scoring *U-35* claimed no fewer than 224 in its wartime career. Yet the decision quickly rebounded on them when following the newly adopted policy – sink all ships bound for British ports without prior warning – five American vessels went under in quick succession. Public opinion was incensed, and the stage was set for a belated US entry into the war on 6 April. The first British naval convoy set sail on 10 May. Only by such convoys and improvements in listening devices and depth charges could the Allies successfully counter the U-Boat menace.

The Russian Revolution began on 12 March, the previous month having seen a combination of adverse weather conditions and fuel/food shortages reduce morale to rock bottom. As rationing was imposed, factory workers in the capital of Petrograd (now Leningrad) rioted, while troops sent to quell the disturbance joined the insurrection. Rebellion spread like wildfire and the Tsar abdicated in March. He and his family were later murdered.

On the Western Front, 9 April saw a successful British assault on Arras. The Canadians captured Vimy Ridge on the 10th with casualties nearing 10,000 but these gains were negated when the hopelessly optimistic French Nivelle Offensive foundered. Planned against German positions on the River Aisne but carried out against the well-defended Hindenburg Line the Germans had withdrawn to in March, the aftermath saw Nivelle replaced by General Pétain and mutiny in large sections of the French Army.

Lenin arrived in Russia from exile on 16 April to take up his position as leader of the Communist Bolsheviks; his arrival sowed the seeds for the so-called October Revolution later in the year.

The early months of 1917 had gone badly for the British Royal Flying Corps, culminating in 'Bloody April' as outclassed British machines and inexperienced pilots were blasted from the sky in ever-increasing numbers, by the highly capable German Albatros DVa. Life expectancy of an RFC pilot on the Western Front lay between 11 days and three weeks.

Daylight fixed-wing bombing raids on Britain began on 25 May when Gotha bombers attacked the Channel port of Folkestone. Like the Zeppelins before them, Germany's Gotha and Giant bombers were capable of destruction on a minor scale (some 835 dead and 1972 injured), but were sufficient to inspire the building of the Handley Page 0/400 and V/1500, long range bombers prevented by peace from retaliating in kind.

The British attack on the Messines Ridge on 7 June was successful, raising hopes of a quick and emphatic victory in the 3rd Battle of Ypres. It was not to be. The British attacked the

Previous page: British troops pose happily for the camera in a captured German trench in March 1917.

Left: Belgian armored cars and their crews at Houthem in September 1917.

Right: Fighting in the streets during the Russian Revolution.

Germans on a battlefield turned into a quagmire by heavy rain. The Allies advanced less than five miles in five months, losing almost a quarter of a million men in the process to German defenders bolstered by a new hazard – reinforced concrete pillboxes which proved costly to take. Passchendaele finally fell on 7 November, ending the Battle of Ypres at last but at the cost of 245,000 British and 8500 French casualties.

The Kerensky offensive of 1 July, when Russian forces massed in strength to fight the Austrians in Galicia, was the final war effort from that country. Some 200,000 men were brought to a halt after a first promising week of fighting, and the subsequent disintegration of the Russian Army set the scene for the Bolshevik Revolution. War-weariness had hit the nation, and as Germany took the Baltic port of Riga in September it was clear the writing was on the wall. The Eastern Front held no longer.

Back in the West, massed tanks, combined with 'predicted shooting', proved a potent weapon for the British in the Battle of Cambrai on 20 November. 476 of the 25-tonne machines proved enormously successful in pushing the German Hindenburg Line back four miles and proved the tank to be a potent weapon capable of turning the ground war decisively in the Allies' favor. They were to play a part in all the major battles of the war's last year, but by the end of the first day at Cambrai half of them were unserviceable and in the ensuing trench warfare the gains were given up.

The Austro-German attack on the Italians at Caporetto on 24 October was shrewdly judged, aimed as it was for the weakest part of the Italian lines manned by ex-factory workers serving as punishment for attempting to start an insurrection. They predictably fled, the remainder of the Italian forces falling back north of Venice to the River Piave. In the earlier battles on the Isonzo, the Italians had sustained 600,000 casualties.

The Bolshevik Revolution of November 1917, confusingly known as the October Revolution (the Russians operating on the Julian calendar), was achieved with few casualties as a nation tired of war opted for 'Peace, Land and Bread' offered by Lenin and Trotsky. Lenin had been permitted to return from exile in Switzerland by the German high command, crossing German territory in a sealed train, in April. Negotiations began for a peace the Germans clearly intended not to honor (an Armistice between Russia and the Central Powers was signed on 17 December), though events in the west would deflect them from greatly extending their gains.

The year ended well for the British in the Middle East: with the capture of Jerusalem, the capital of Palestine on 9 December. The efforts of T E Lawrence, popularly known as Lawrence of Arabia, persuading the Arab tribesmen to assist the Allied cause by turning against the Turks had at last borne fruit but the main effort had been by conventional forces led by General Allenby.

Below: A rudimentary mule-drawn sleigh carries Allied supplies over a muddy area on the Balkan Front, January 1917.

Right: General Sir George Milne confers with General Mishitch at Salonika, January 1917. As well as the British and Serbian units they commanded, the Allied forces at Salonika included Greek, French and Italian troops.

Bottom: Bulgarian infantry trenches facing the British forces at Salonika, 1917. Two and one half million British and Empire troops were tied up by actions in the Middle East, and in this regard the Bulgarians and Turks were assisting the German war effort.

Left: The French '75' was the best field gun of the war, with an impressive firing rate of six rounds per minute. It was less successful in trench warfare, however, where less maneuverable, larger-caliber guns held sway.

Below: A French 220mm mortar in battlefield action. Trenches were designed to withstand anything but a direct hit, but clearly limited soldiers' mobility.

Bottom: St Chamond tanks passing through the village of Condé-sur-Aisne. Tanks were notable in all the major battles of the last year of the war and were later admitted by the supreme German commander to have been a decisive factor in his country's defeat.

Left: General Robert Nivelle, who replaced Joffre as French Commander-in-Chief in 1916, had been a successful artillery officer at Verdun, but his plan for a major offensive, carried out in April 1917, to combine an artillery barrage with a surprise infantry attack broke down within hours when the attacking troops became bogged down in the shortened German front line. Instead of bringing a loudly-promised victory, he brought the French Army to the edge of revolt and was soon himself replaced by General Pétain.

Below: A French sniper uses telescopic sights on his rifle in the trenches in the Tracy lé Val area (Oise), February 1917.

Top right: French troops hurry through communication trenches to reinforce frontline positions.

Bottom right: Camouflaged French heavy artillery mounted on a railway wagon in action near Vienne-le-Chateau on the Marne.

Left: An officer of the 10th Scottish Rifles leads his men over the top as shells burst around them, 24 March 1917.

Top: The band of the 5th Australian Infantry Brigade (2nd Australian Division) plays on in shell-torn Bapaume while the town is still smouldering, March 1917.

Above left: A night patrol leaves an Allied trench in camouflage snow suits, Cambrai, 12 January 1917.

Above right: General Sir Henry Rawlinson, commander of the British Fourth Army, is pictured in conversation with M Babin, a French war correspondent, at Peronne, March 1917.

Above: John Singer Sargent's painting 'Gassed'. These men, like most other cases of the 1918 battles, were victims of mustard gas.

Left: Concealed under camouflage netting, a British 12-inch howitzer pounds enemy positions around Arras, April 1917.

Right: Infantry fix scaling ladders in preparation for leaving their trenches on the day before the Battle of Arras, 8 April 1917. The British attack was intended to divert German attention from the Nivelle Offensive – a push to the River Aisne - which was to follow shortly.

Above: The 12th King's Liverpool Regiment pictured with trophies captured during the Battle of Arras, 10 April 1917. Behind them is a German mobile 'pill-box' and a concrete observation tower.

Left: Infantryman of the Australian Army inspect a trench mortar position in a waterlogged trench. Mortars were an important source of firepower for front-line troops but were unpopular because of the enemy retaliation they inevitably quickly attracted.

Top right: British armored cars are pictured in a battle-damaged street in Arras, April 1917.

Bottom right: 18-pound artillery pieces are deployed on newly-won ground near Feuchy crossroads during the Battle of Arras as infantry come down from the line and a tank goes up. Note the abandoned communications trench with its corrugated iron roof and waterproof-sheet ends.

Top left: 'Over the Top' by Paul Nash. This painting depicted an actual event, a small attack at Marcoing in December 1917 by 1st Artists' Rifles.

Bottom left: The German retrenchment to the Hindenburg Line (or *Siegfried Stellung*) was less a retreat than a shrewd tactical withdrawal. British and French troops are here pictured in reserve lines at Le Verquier, 25 April 1917, following the German move.

Above: Australian troops study a large contour map to give them a good knowledge of the country over which they were to press home their attack. The Allied victory at Messines was assisted by strategic explosions involving nearly a million pound weight of high explosive.

Right: Frontline British troops board commandeered buses in Arras for a period of rest and recuperation, May 1917.

Bottom right: A ration party of a Scottish Regiment passing through the ruins of Beaucourt, 26 May 1917, with plenty of the famed Flanders mud in evidence.

Left: Kaiser Wilhelm II visits his troops to bestow decorations, June 1917. A grandson of Queen Victoria, he ruled Germany from 1888 to 1918: the British press scornfully called him 'Kaiser Bill'.

Below left: A German truck-mounted anti-aircraft gun in action, Flanders, August 1917.

Right: A crowded road at Fricourt as pioneers continue their road-widening efforts to accommodate staffcars, mule-drawn casualty limbers, trucks, an ambulance and marching infantry.

Below: A battery of 155mm artillery pieces in an advanced position near Froissy, July 1917.

Left: German balloon observers parachute to safety. While tethered balloons were widely used for observation purposes, they were by no means immune to aerial attack, as British scouts here illustrate.

Below: German Albatros Type DII biplanes are prepared for flight. These sleek, shark-like scouts allied good performance with twin machine-gun armament – twice the firepower most British aircraft of the time could boast.

Above right: German anti-aircraft machine gunners.

Below right: Italy's three-engined Caproni bipiane bombers (the Ca 5 illustrated) proved first-class machines in the service of both their home country and France. From modest beginnings, the bomber emerged by the end of the war as a weapon with enormous strategic and tactical potential.

Far right: Baron Manfred von Richthofen, Germany's most feared scout pilot, who died with 80 confirmed combat victories to his credit.

Bottom right: German air power in large and small sizes: a twin-engined Gotha heavy bomber and a single-seat Albatros scout as escort. The later Albatros variants, known as 'Vee-strutters' to the Allies for obvious reasons, were greatly feared while the Gotha succeeded the vulnerable Zeppelins in bombing raids on Britain.

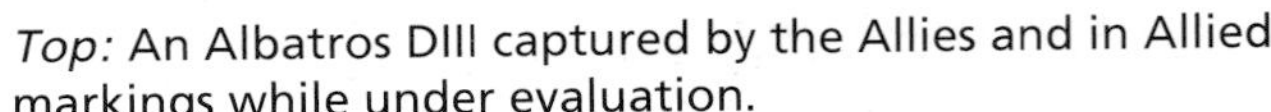

Top: An Albatros DIII captured by the Allies and in Allied markings while under evaluation.

Above left: Captain Baron Manfred von Richthofen's pursuit flight on the Western Front. When given command of his own fighter squadron, Jagdstaffel 11, he was allowed to choose many of the members, among whom was his brother Lothar.

Above: Members of the 6th Australian Squadron, Royal Flying Corps, prepare for a night bombing raid in their de Havilland DH-4.

Right: Albatros biplanes of Baron von Richthofen's circus, May 1917. Richthofen's own aircraft was painted red, hence his popular soubriquet of 'Red Baron'.

Far left: British fighter ace Captain Albert Ball, who won the Victoria Cross.

Left: French fighter pilot Lieutenant Charles Nungesser, pictured beside his Nieuport biplane. He brought down 45 German aeroplanes to end the war his country's third-ranking ace and – crucially – the top-scoring survivor.

Bottom left: The Queen with General Trenchard, commander of the RFC and later the RAF, inspects Bristol Fighter-equipped unit of the RFC at St Omer, July 1917.

Right: Having fought as part of the French air force, Escadrille N 124 Lafayette was reconstituted as the 103rd Aero Squadron of the US Army Air Corps after that country's official entry into the war in April 1917.

Below: With its powerful rotary engine, the British Sopwith Camel scout was a hard aircraft to master, but the exploits of those who succeeded helped it become the top-scoring scout of the war on either side.

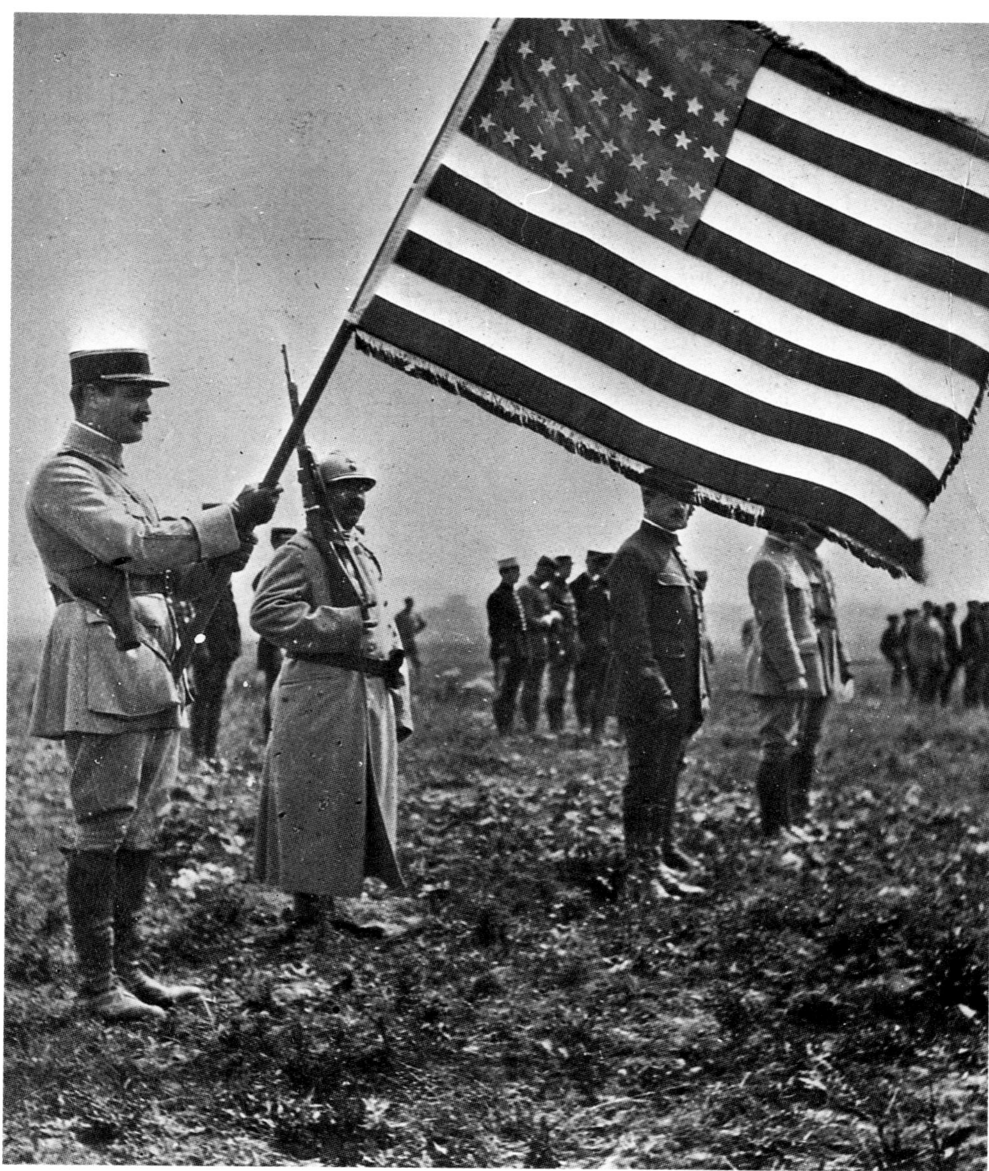

INCORRECT METHOD.
THE NATURAL INCLINATION OF THE ATTACKER, IF INEXPERIENCED, IS TO TURN IN THE SAME DIRECTION AND FOLLOW.
THIS RESULTS IN GIVING THE ENEMY JUST THE OPPORTUNITY HE DESIRES.
1ST POSITION
ATTACKING MACHINE DIRECTLY BEHIND & BELOW OPPONENT.
1ST POSITION
ENEMY'S GUN UNABLE TO BEAR ON SCOUT.
2ND POSITION
SCOUT FOILS ENEMY'S ATTEMPT BY IMMEDIATE TURN IN OPPOSITE DIRECTION.
2ND POSITION
ENEMY MACHINE BANKING IN AN ATTEMPT TO BRING HIS GUN TO BEAR ON SCOUT
3RD POSITION
REGAINS FAVOURABLE ATTACKING POSITION BY TURNING TOWARDS ENEMY.
3RD POSITION
ENEMY MACHINE COMING OFF HIS BANK AS MANOEUVRE HAS FAILED.
4TH POSITION
ATTACKING MACHINE AGAIN IN POSITION UNDER ENEMY'S TAIL.
4TH POSITION
ENEMY'S GUN AGAIN UNABLE TO BEAR ON SCOUT.
A HOSTILE TWO-SEATER WHEN ATTACKED FROM BEHIND AND BELOW ALMOST INVARIABLY TURNS WITH A VIEW TO BRINGING THE OBSERVER'S GUN TO BEAR ON THE ATTACKER.
THIS MANOEUVRE CAN BE EFFECTIVELY COUNTERED BY TURNING AT FIRST IN THE OPPOSITE DIRECTION AND THEN, TAKING ADVANTAGE OF SUPERIOR SPEED AND HANDINESS, TURNING AFTER THE ENEMY AND AGAIN COMING UNDER HIS TAIL.
This diagram is the property of H.M. Government and is intended for Official use only.

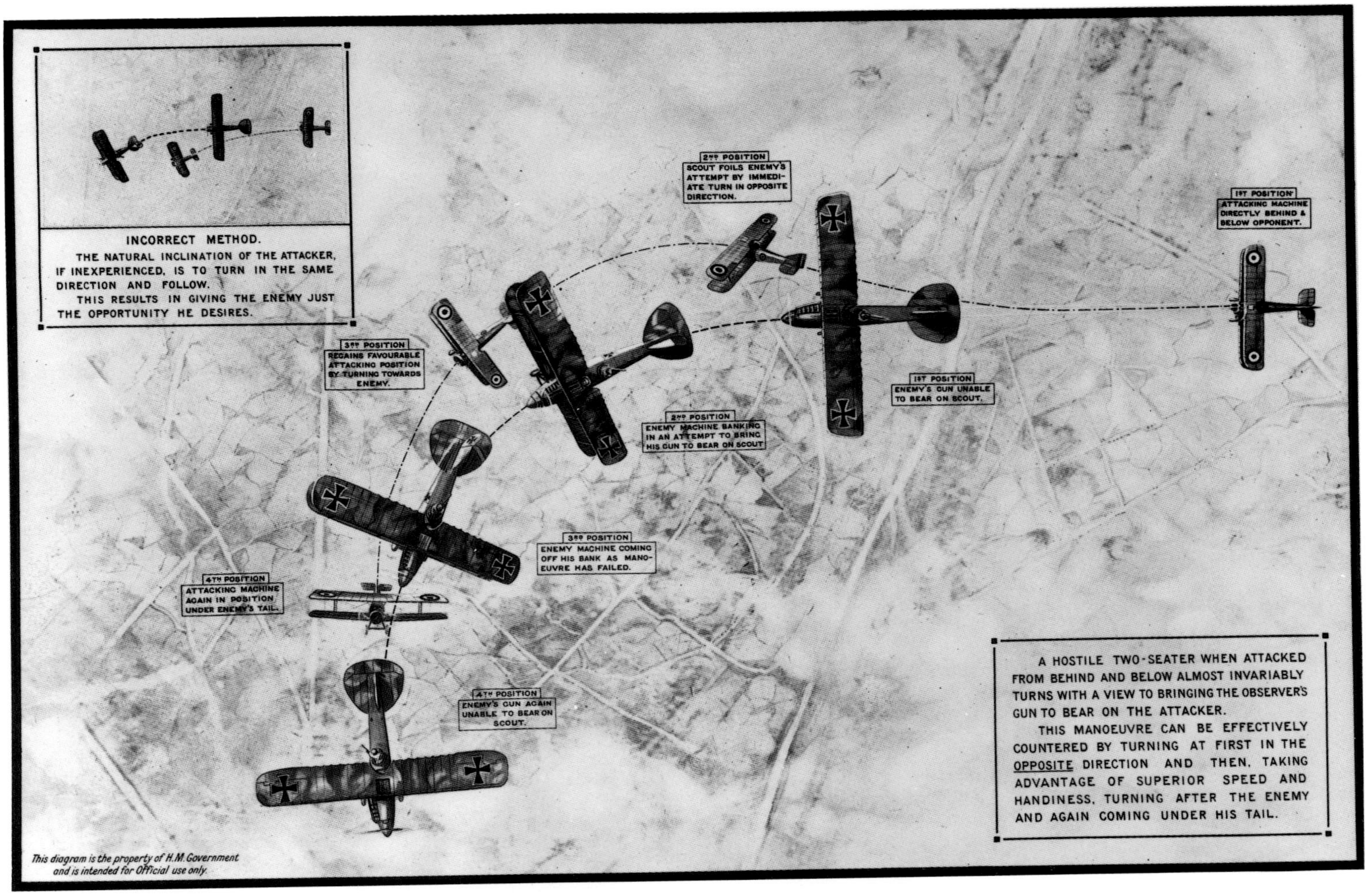

Top left: Dogfighting was in its infancy, and airmen frequently had to learn through bitter experience. This diagram shows the right way to attack a two-seater with flexibly-mounted rearward-facing machine gun – approaching from behind and below in the 'shadow' of the tailplane where the gun cannot be brought to bear.

Left: A Royal Flying Corps groundcrewman fits an aerial camera to a two-seat reconnaissance type beside the observer's cockpit. Though fighter aces grabbed the glory, reconnaissance remained the most vital role for the air arms of both sides.

Above: The German U-boat *U-35* runs on the surface before submerging, 1917. By the war's end, *U-35*'s exploits had made it the most successful submarine of all time, claiming 224 victims in the Mediterranean.

Above: The British battleship *Warspite*, showing evidence of early countermeasures – in this case, jagged strips of canvas attached to its funnels in order to disguise their shape and make it difficult for enemy range-finders to fix the position and course of their target.

Left: As London came under aerial attack from Zeppelins and, later, Gotha and Giant fixed-wing bombers, countermeasures such as a wire apron suspended from barrage balloons were improvised to ensnare the intruders who often attacked at night.

Top left: This view of the torpedo room of a German submarine gives some measure of the claustrophobic conditions in which sub crews operated.

Bottom left: German submarines *U-35* (nearest camera) and the smaller *U-42* meet at a pre-arranged Mediterranean rendezvous point, April-May 1917.

Above: The Italian dreadnought *Guilio Cesare*, pictured at Taranto, 3 June 1917.

Right: German naval ratings receive and stow away torpedoes on board a submarine during a high seas rendezvous.

Left: Record-breaking U-boat *U-35* claims another of her 224 Allied victims with a torpedo strike. Invincible and undetectable at the beginning of the war, the undersea menace was gradually overhauled by advances in technology.

Below: This picture of the crew of a German submarine on deck gives some idea of the size of these craft as compared with their better-known World War II successors.

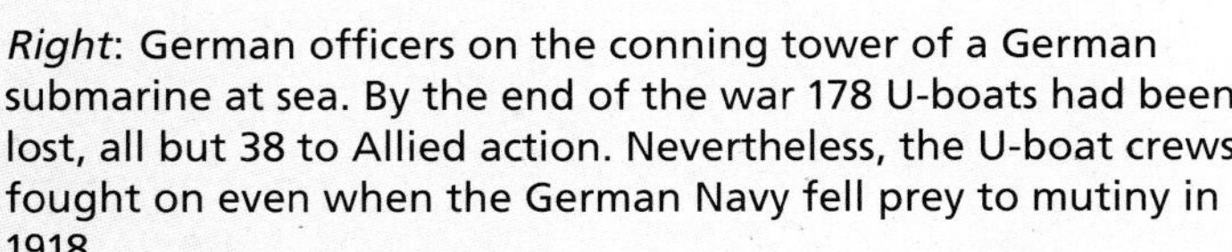

Right: German officers on the conning tower of a German submarine at sea. By the end of the war 178 U-boats had been lost, all but 38 to Allied action. Nevertheless, the U-boat crews fought on even when the German Navy fell prey to mutiny in 1918.

Far right: A small submarine of the UB type alongside *U-35* in the Mediterranean. The figure on the right in British military uniform is King's Messenger Captain Wilson, taken prisoner by the *U-35*.

Top left: Men of the York and Lancs Regiment on the 62nd Division front at Oppy-Gavrelle take up wire for a night working party to reinforce trench defenses.

Bottom left: Stacks of Allied rations at Rouen, 15 January 1917, evidence of the massive logistic support required to keep the armies fighting.

Right: The Queen inspects representatives of the South African Native Labour Corps at Abbeville, June 1917.

Below: Souvenirs of battle are displayed by men of the Inniskilling Fusiliers after the capture of Wytschaete, 11 June 1917 during the Battle of Messines. Objects on view include bayonets, rifles, Maxim machine guns, entrenching tools and helmets – especially the decorated 'Pickelhaube' variety, usually (but not here) seen with spike.

Top left: British soldiers take a welcome break from the mud and grime of the trenches to bathe in the pond of a farm near St Eloi, 10 June 1917.

Bottom left: A Portuguese gas sentry stands beside a rudimentary rocket launcher, used to give warning of attack, in the trenches near Neuve Chapelle, 24 June 1917.

Below: German artillerymen advance to the front line. Note that both men and horses wear gas masks.

Right: Even when out of the trenches at rest soldiers' accommodation was often scarcely luxurious. 'Rest' too was often a misnomer, involving arduous road construction or supply transport work.

Bottom: The Kaiser presents medals to a group of German soldiers.

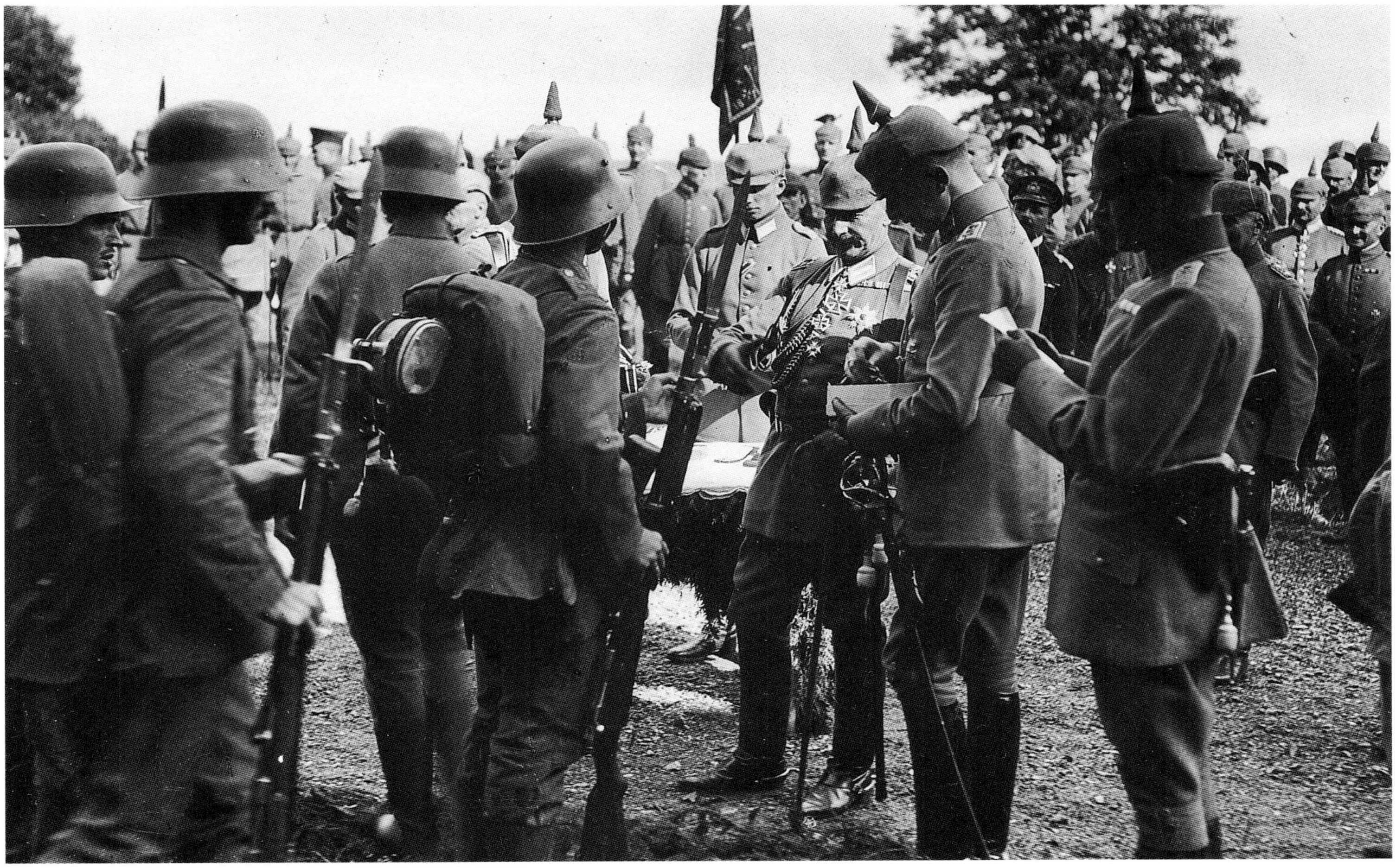

Left: General Sir Henry Horne, Commander of the British First Army, pictured with his charger at the First Army Horse Show at the Chateau de la Haie, June 1917. Along with fellow commanders Generals Plumer (Second) and Allenby (Third), Horne was to distinguish himself in the battles to come.

Below: Royal Engineers bridge the Yser Canal, north of Ypres, 3 August 1917, using an old barge as their foundation.

Right: Battles of Ypres. The 7th Northamptonshire Regiment make camp near Dickebusch, 9 August 1917, resting after an attack on 31 July in which they lost their commanding officer, 11 officers and 246 men.

Bottom right: A parade of Chinese laborers at Boulogne, August 1917. Many thousands of such workers were brought to France from the Allied colonies for construction service behind the lines.

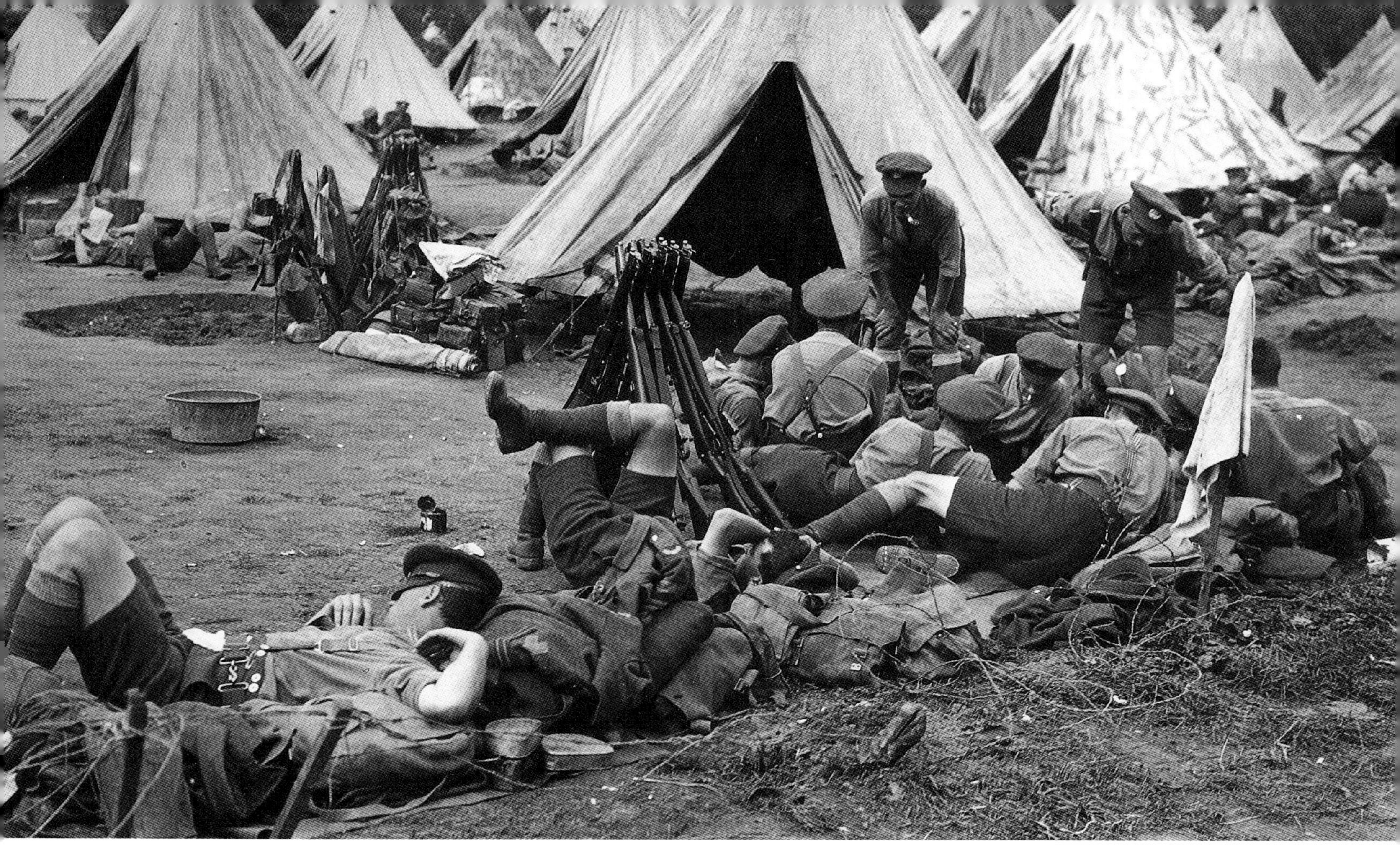

Right: Shell burst in the ruins of Boesinghe Station during the Battle of Langemarck, August 1917. The remains of a train can be seen in the distance. Old railway materials were used in the building of the (now destroyed) trench in the foreground.

Below: Belgian soldiers in the front line clean kit and equipment, 9 September 1917.

Bottom: A battery of Australian heavy artillery makes ready for action in the Ypres sector, 12 September 1917. 8-inch howitzers like these were mainly responsible for the destruction of Flanders' delicate drainage system.

Left: Indian Lancers lead the advance across the Jebel Hamrin, Palestine, 1917, where they faced the Turks.

Below: British forces enter Jerusalem, November 1917. Following the repulse of attacks in the Second Battle of Gaza in April, General Edmund Allenby took over the British force and his well-designed attack in October broke through to Jerusalem.

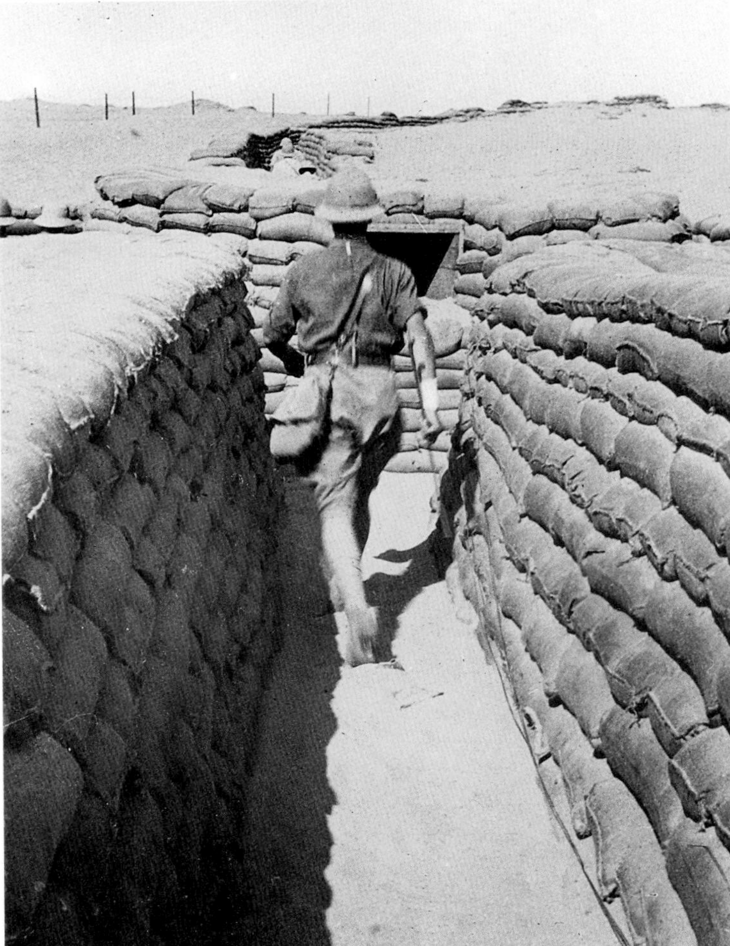

Above: Communications in Palestine were almost totally non-existent before 1915-16. Here, British troops lay railroad track across the Sinai Desert.

Left: The British trenches at Samsons Ridge, Gaza, Palestine in the summer of 1917.

Top right: The Emir Feisal and his elite bodyguard, a hand-picked band of camel-mounted tribesmen.

Bottom right: The Imperial Camel Corps Brigade outside Beershaba, November 1917. The British Army had drawn on its experiences in the colonies to utilise every available source of animal transport.

Left: Part of the railway raiding party led by Lawrence during the Arab Revolt.

Right: Emir Feisal whose resistance was inspired by Lawrence.

Far right: Sent to Arabia as a British intelligence officer to assess the Arab revolt, Colonel TE Lawrence went on to become a renowned guerrilla leader and desert legend.

Below: Tribal representatives advance under the cover of the white flag to swear allegiance to the Emir Feisal at Akaba.

Below: General von Falkenhayn (second left) and staff conversing with a Turkish officer, Palestine Front. The veteran Falkenhayn was commander of the Central Powers' forces in Palestine.

Right: General Allenby's official entry into Jerusalem, 11 December 1917, was considered a 'Christmas present' for Lloyd George and marked a successful end to a generally disappointing year. The city had little strategic value, but its capture was something of a propaganda coup.

Bottom: Troopers of the 14th (Kings) Hussars resting on the way back from an action against the Turks at Jebel Hamrin, December 1917. Cavalry played a significant role in the Palestine campaign.

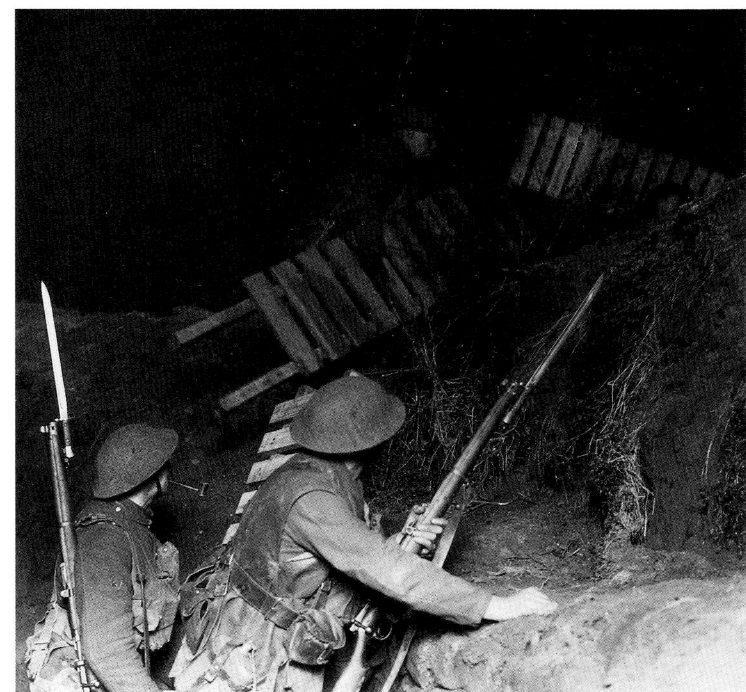

Right: A fatigue party take their duckboards over a support line trench at night at Cambrai, January 1917.

Below: Lancashire Fusiliers use a hand pump to drain a front-line trench opposite Messines, near Ploegsteert Wood, January 1917.

Top left: The Queen of the Belgians visits her country's troops at the Front, 1917. Despite their early setbacks when their country was occupied, the re-equipped Belgians fought side-by-side with British and French troops in the later stages of the conflict.

Bottom left: British troops prepare to fire a 9.45-inch heavy trench mortar in a captured German trench in Pigeon Wood, Gommecourt, March 1917.

Top right: HM the King of the Belgians at work in his headquarters, 1917.

Right: A carefully camouflaged German gun battery near Ostend.

Below: A Belgian machine gun section makes its way to the front-line trenches.

Far left: Attending to the Allied wounded at an advanced dressing station near Ypres, September 1917.

Left: A woebegone German prisoner captured in the attack on Vampire Farm, near Potijze, by Scottish and South African troops during the Battle of Menin Road Ridge, September 1917.

Above: Stretcher bearers near Zilloteke, 21 September 1917.

Above: Field Marshal Sir Douglas Haig on horseback, September 1917.

Below: A German automatic gun battery at Zeebrugge on the Flanders coast. By 1917 ports on the Flanders coast had become U-Boat bases and clearing these was a major objective for the British attacks in 1917.

Left: Camouflaged tanks and infantry moving up to the attack as shells burst in the distance during the Battle of Polygon Wood on the Menin Road 3 miles east of Ypres, 26 September 1917.

Bottom left: An Australian soldier of I Anzac Corps receives his issue of clean underwear at Ypres, October 1917.

Right: Two British soldiers take a meal break seemingly oblivious to the destruction wrought around them by artillery, Flanders, 1917.

Below: A pair of 9.2 inch howitzers at Guillemont await the order to fire, 4 October 1917. They have been sited in a rather exposed position.

Left: Despite the winter cold, physical exercises remain mandatory at this Allied Training Camp. The British forces maintained a training camp at Etaples where harsh discipline and physical training were the norm. This was especially resented by the many troops returning to units after being wounded, especially since many instructors had seen no front-line service. A more constructive regime was established after a 'mutiny' at Etaples later in 1917.

Bottom left: Anzac road-makers enjoy a brief respite and a midday meal. Initially in evidence at Gallipoli, troops from Australia and New Zealand acquitted themselves honorably on the Western Front and elsewhere as the war continued.

Right: An Anzac writes a letter home from his billet on the Western Front.

Below: Men of the Royal Engineers take a telephone wire up to the Front between Pilcken and Langemarck, 10 October 1917.

Bottom: A mule team of the 1st Anzac Corps gets stuck in the mud beyond recovery at Polejze Farm, 19 October 1917.

Top left: Men of the 15th Royal Welch Fusiliers (London Welsh) fill sandbags with the earth excavated in the construction of a dug-out in their trenches at Fleurbaix, 28 December 1917.

Left: The Menin Road, Ypres, during the winter of 1917-18, said to be the worst in living memory.

Top right: German troops pick their way through the shell holes. The damage done by both sides to the Flanders battleground would take decades to repair.

Right: A German is taken prisoner near Havrincourt during the Battle of Cambrai, 20 November 1917.

Top left: German storm troops train for the Battle of Caporetto. Fought in October 1917, the Italian defenses were torn apart by crack German and Austrian soldiers who took 275,000 prisoners and 2500 guns.

Left: Italian troops march two abreast either side of the road. With hundreds of thousands of Italians deserting at Caporetto, Allied hopes of outright victory took a severe blow.

Top: Italian troops at the Piave River 60 miles from Caporetto, where French and British divisions came to their aid from the Western Front.

Above: General Cadorna (center) pictured on horseback while crossing the Dolomites. Ironically it was Austrian appeals for help following Cadorna's attacks in the Eleventh Battle of the Isonzo in August 1917 which brought the Germans to Italy and led to Cadorna's defeat at Caporetto.

Right: Italian commander General Cadorna. The Italian collapse within three weeks at Caporetto followed 600,000 battlefield casualties sustained in the series of battles along the Isonzo River.

Top left: Troops on the Italian Front board a truck in the shadow of the Dolomite mountains. By October 1917, the Germans had depleted their personnel on the Western Front in favor of pursuing campaigns elsewhere.

Above: Austrian soldiers in a well dug trench on the Italian Front.

Top right: The German advance into Italy continues.

Right: German flame throwers in action.

Left: Fully-laden German troops on the road after the Battle of Caporetto. The men in the truck are some of the many Italian prisoners taken in an action that cost the Italians 165,000 men.

Bottom left: German trucks advance through Cividale.

Below: German troops take a well-earned break after their victorious exploits at Caporetto.

Right: An Italian gun and one of its late crew are graphically pictured after a direct hit during the Isonzo fighting.

Bottom: A working party of the 1st Battalion South Staffordshire Regiment, 7th Division, digs trenches on a mountainside on the Italian Front. British and French troops were quickly sent to Italy to help the Italians after Caporetto.

Top left: General Oscar von Hutier (left), pictured at the Battle of Riga which his tactic of 'predicted shooting' – opening fire unannounced at an estimated range without first using sighting shots – did much to win.

Left: Russian Minister of War Alexander Kerensky, pictured in his cabinet room shortly after the formation of the Provisional Government, 1917.

Below: August von Mackensen, recently promoted to the rank of Field Marshal, inspects the troops that captured Bucharest in December 1916.

Top right: By 1917, the war-weary Russians were ready to make peace with their invaders, but the agreement imposed by the Germans in conference at Brest Litovsk was very harsh in its terms.

Bottom right: Captured Russian trenches and barbed wire defenses captured by the Austro-German Army in the Battle of East Galicia, 24 July 1917.

Left: The monk Rasputin whose influence over the Tsarina and hence Russian policy was a source of conflict within the Russian leadership up to the time of his assassination in 1916.

Below: German troops disembark at Riga, the Baltic Port taken by General von Hutier's Eighth Army in a surprise attack in September-October 1917. A German transport ship and a seaplane are visible in the background.

Top right: The public read newsheets issued by the Duma after the first 1917 Revolution in Petrograd.

Bottom right: A street scene in June 1917 during the period of the Provisional Government. Founded after the February Revolution, it was unseated in November by the Bolsheviks.

ОХТЕНСКIЙ ПОРОХОВОЙ ЗАВ.
ДА ЗДРАВСТВУЕТЪ ПРАЗДНИКЪ ТРУДА
СТАРО-НЕВСК

Far left: Lenin speaks in Moscow, 7 November 1918. The Bolshevik leader was the dominant force in wartime Russian politics.

Left: A tram is taken over and used as a barricade by Communist supporters in Moscow during street fighting in November 1917.

Right: Austrian Foreign Minister Count Czernin (*left*) and his German counterpart von Kuhlmann arrive at Brest-Litovsk for the Peace Conference with Russia, 20 December 1917. With the might of the German Army behind them, they were clearly in a position to dictate terms.

Below: Germans fire at the retreating Bolsheviks in early 1918.

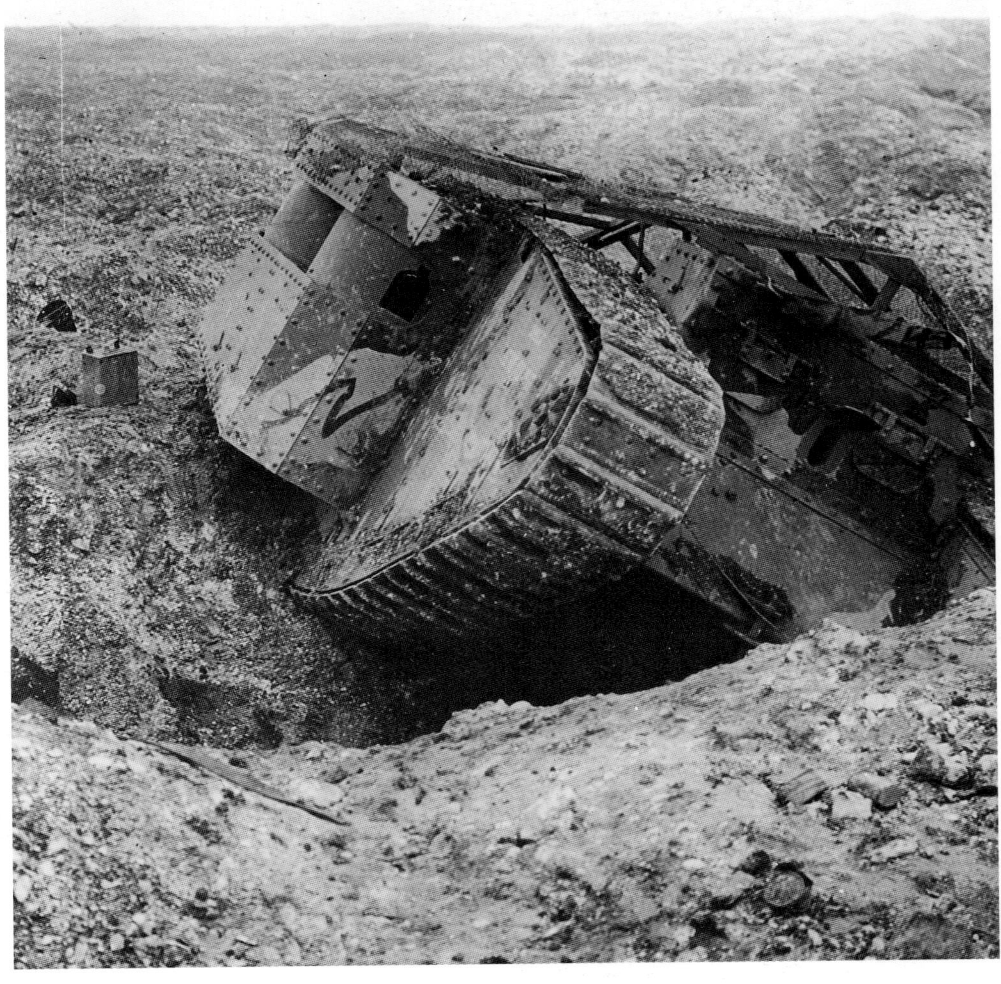

Left: Early wartime tanks lacked both maneuverability and reliability. This tank was lost from British front-line strength when it fell into a shell-hole at the Battle of Ypres, 1917.

Bottom left: Colonel J F C Fuller, chief British theorist of tank warfare. Tanks were active in every major battle of the last year of the war, scoring their first major success at Cambrai in November 1917.

Below: The 'Blue Front Bar' advertises its prices on an improvised notice board.

Right: Men of the 11th Leicester Regiment (6th Division) armed with machine guns pictured in a captured second-line trench at Ribecourt during the Battle of Cambrai, 20 November 1917.

Bottom right: A British tank brings in a captured German 5.9-inch gun at the Battle of Cambrai, November 1917. In 12 hours, with only light casualties, 476 tanks forced the German line back 10,000 metres – a similar, far more costly gain elsewhere had taken three months. German counterattacks soon wiped out most of the gains, however.

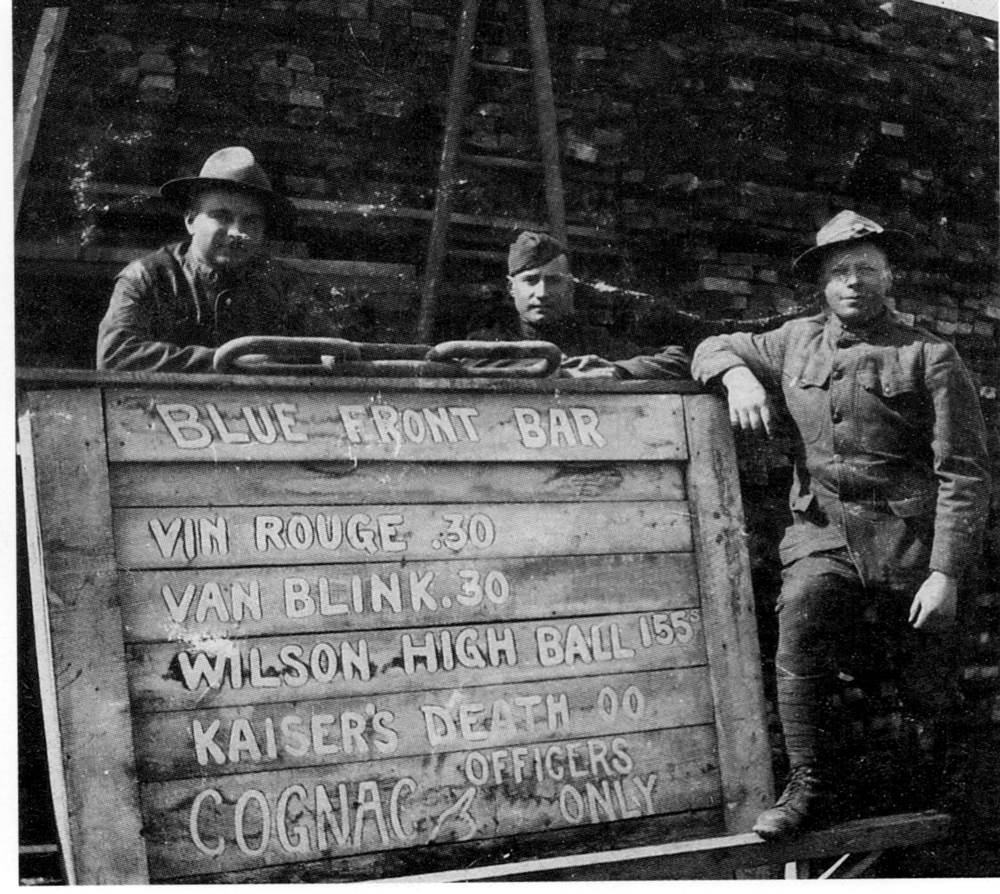

1918

US President Wilson announced a 14-point Peace Plan on 8 January – but like its predecessor it was not well received. Both sides went into the last year of the war in a poor state but neither would give way, though it was evident that the imminent arrival in Europe of American forces in great numbers would soon tip the scales on the Western Front in the Allies' favor.

With this very much in mind, the Germans planned an all-out attack – this was Operation Michael, intended to beat the build-up of the American Expeditionary Force under General Pershing. Part of their plan was to employ highly trained 'stormtroopers' similar to those who had proved so effective at Caporetto to keep the all-important momentum of battle going, bypassing blockages on the battlefield by means of infiltration tactics and causing alarm and despondency behind enemy lines. This was to be combined with greater use of 'predicted shooting', placing considerable emphasis on secrecy in the positioning of artillery.

59 German divisions of three armies were to be employed on the offensive, supported by the largest artillery force ever assembled: 6473 artillery pieces and 3532 trench mortars. The assembled barrage duly opened up in the small hours of 21 March – and proved both spectacular and effective. The British lines were broken and the Germans advanced 40 miles in a week – but the Allies retreated in good order. They made the opposition fight all the way and casualties were by no means one-sided. Looting began when the Germans overran British supply dumps, symptomatic of a breakdown of discipline, while the key city of Amiens remained out of reach in Allied hands.

The Germans planned a second artillery-led blow – Operation George, further north at the River Lys – but this failed to achieve lasting gains after early spectacular advances. Greater success was achieved against the French at the Third Battle of the Aisne, and by 3 June the Germans had once more reached the River Marne. But they were now vulnerable to counter-attack and the Second Battle of the Marne saw the Allies take the initiative. They were not to lose it again.

A quarter of a million US troops landed in Europe during June. July 15 saw the last German attack on the Marne, while the Allied push at Amiens on 8 August – the 'black day of the German Army', according to General Ludendorff – saw a bombardment of predicted shooting catch the Germans at their own game. But this time the result was different: the German Army, now fatally demoralised after the failure to break through, tore like paper and the Allied advance from here on proved unstoppable. The Americans weighed in with a victory at St Mihiel, and the final breakthrough of the Hindenburg Line on 29 September yielded 35,000 prisoners.

History had earlier been made with warfare's first all-tank action, fought in March between three British Mark IV

machines and a German A7V. Two of the British vehicles were only machine-gun armed, and retreated leaving their compatriot armed with two six-pound guns to take on the A7V's 57mm weapon. It scored four hits, after which the German machine toppled over on attempting to retreat and was abandoned by its crew. The design was noticeably unstable due to the top-heavy mounting of its gun.

1 April 1918 saw the official combination of Britain's Royal Flying Corps and Royal Naval Air Service into the Royal Air Force, the world's first independent air force – recognition that air power was here to stay. By the end of the war it had grown into the largest and most capable air force anywhere in the world, with some 22,000 machines and nearly 300,000 officers and men.

Superior scouts like the SE 5A had tipped the balance in the Allies' favor in the final months, while only the Armistice was to prevent the Handley Page V/1500 heavy bomber (only three of which had by then been built) from subjecting Berlin to an early taste of the bombing it endured in the 1939-45 conflict. The seeds of future air warfare had indeed been sown.

In the Middle East, the British capture of Damascus on 1 October was due in no small measure to Arab champion T E Lawrence, whose successful prosecution of a campaign of guerrilla warfare against the Turks in conjunction with Arab leader Emir Feisal had latterly been assisted by armament supplies. But Allied-Arab relations were to hit an all-time low when, despite Lawrence's intervention, postwar divisions of territory proved unfavorable to those who had assisted the British cause.

Austria-Hungary had seemed increasingly isolated as German aid dried up and the Serbs and other dispossessed took fresh heart. Occupied Serbia and Bulgaria were taken by the Allies finally advancing from Salonika under General Franchet d'Esperey in late September: an Italian victory over Austria-Hungary at Vittorio Veneto sealed the war on the Italian Front, following which Turkey and Austria-Hungary capitulated.

The war on the Western Front ended at 11am on 11 November 1918 when Germany signed the Armistice in Marshal Foch's train. Kaiser Wilhelm II had abdicated two days earlier and fled to Holland, Germany being proclaimed a republic in his absence. But though peace had been declared, violence continued within Germany as armed paramilitary groups fought for control.

The Treaty of Versailles, signed on 28 June the following year, redrew the map of Europe, confirming the disintegration of the old Austro-Hungarian Empire and creating Yugoslavia, Czechoslovakia and Poland. But the conditions, restrictions and reparations the Germans were obliged to agree to would help sow the seeds of future discontent that would provide Hitler's Third Reich with a fertile foundation.

Previous page: Troops of the US 7th Division cheer on being given news of the armistice to end the war.

Left: US gunners with a 75mm gun in furious action during the fighting in the St Mihiel salient.

Right: German troops begin their attack in the 'Kaiser's Battle', 21 March 1918.

RENVOYER

Left: French troops prepare a mortar in the trenches near La Ville aux Bois (Aisne), February 1918.

Top right: A routine foot inspection by the Medical Officer of the 12th East Yorkshires in a support trench, January 1918. The ailment known as 'trench foot' (or, more descriptively of long periods in wet conditions, 'immersion foot') could cripple large numbers of soldiers, being particularly prevalent in units whose morale was low and discipline and hygiene standards lax.

Right: Men of the 12th East Yorkshires prime an artillery signal rocket in a trench in the Arieux Sector, January 1918. Such signals from the forward trenches frequently requested support fire to protect their occupants from the advancing enemy.

Below: German troops inspect captured British guns and machinery on the Western Front, March 1918.

Far left: Men of the 20th British Division are bolstered by the 22nd French Division as they cover a road in the Somme region, 25 March 1918. Although French commander Philippe Pétain feared a major attack in his own sector, he eventually sent reinforcements to the British.

Left: A German artillery battery opens up during Operation Michael. In all, 6473 guns and 3532 trench mortars were arrayed along the front line for a surprise attack on 21 March 1918, the intention being to pre-empt American reinforcement of the Allied forces.

Right: Portuguese Medical Corps men pictured near Festubert en route to the front line transport their field kits in a light railway trolley, 16 March 1918.

Below: A mighty 21cm howitzer is hauled to a forward position during preparations for Colonel Brüchmuller's planned artillery barrage, March 1918. Brüchmuller had first come to prominence as the artillery chief for the German attack on Riga whose tactics were developed for the attacks in France in 1918 whose artillery he directed.

Top left: Lewis gunners improvise a defense line during the Battle of the Marne. The picture is probably posed as the unrealistic nature of the position suggests.

Left: British field guns in action during the German Somme offensive, 28 March 1918.

Top: For the series of German offensives in 1918 large numbers of guns were switched by rail from sector to sector.

Above: Allied prisoners are force-marched through a French village.

Top left: A French naval gun mounted on an armored train in action, 5 April 1918.

Middle left: French cavalrymen pass through the village of Hesdin in support of the Allied forces in Flanders, 14 April 1918.

Bottom left: A French armored car acts in support of British troops at Materen during the Battle of the Lys, 14 April 1918.

Top right: A line of Allied soldiers blinded by mustard gas await treatment at an Advanced Dressing Station near Béthune, 10 April 1918.

Bottom right: British dead await burial in a cemetery near Monchy le Preux, 1918. At the War's end, the official figures revealed 947,023 fatalities on the British and Commonwealth side alone.

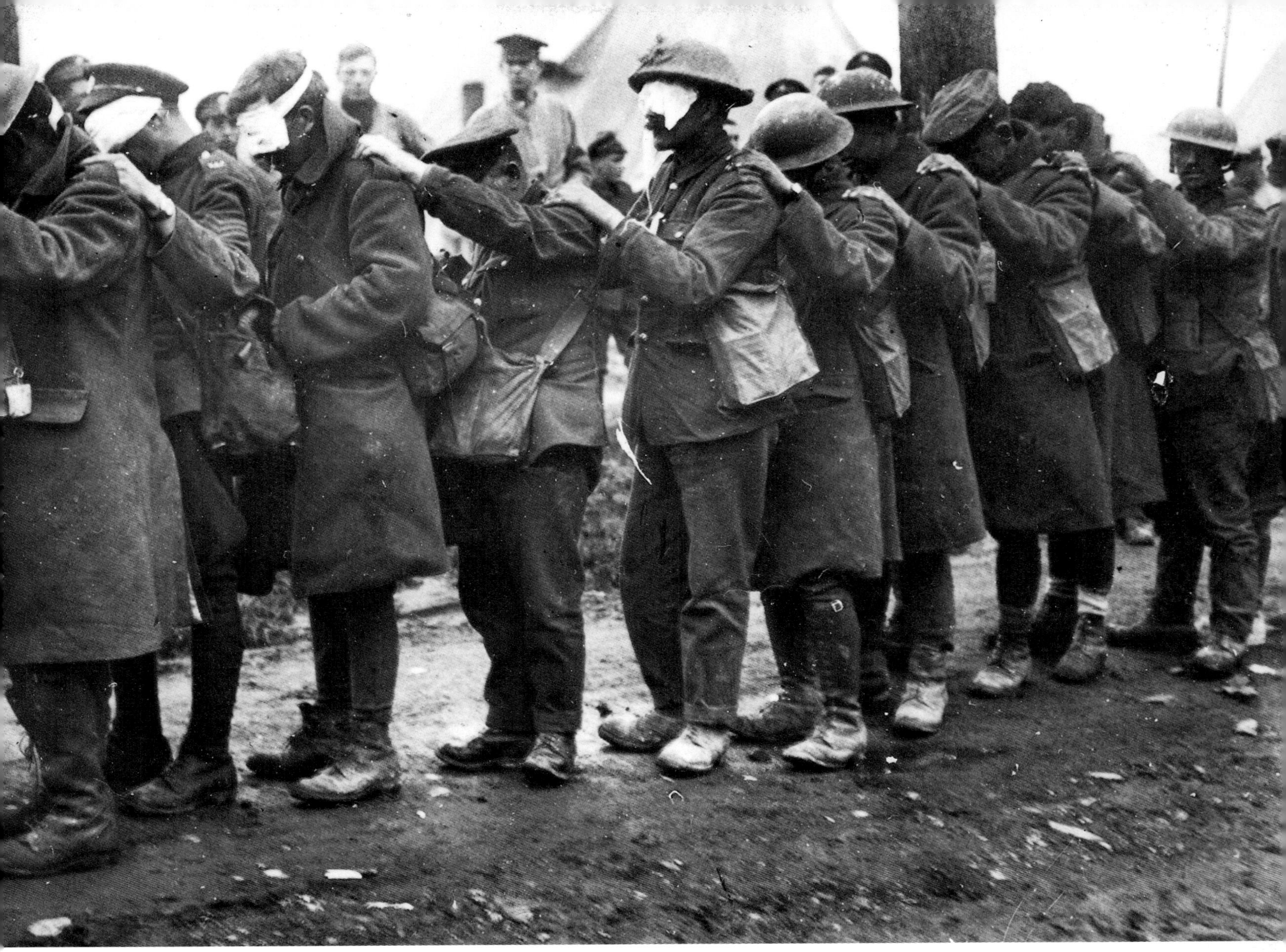

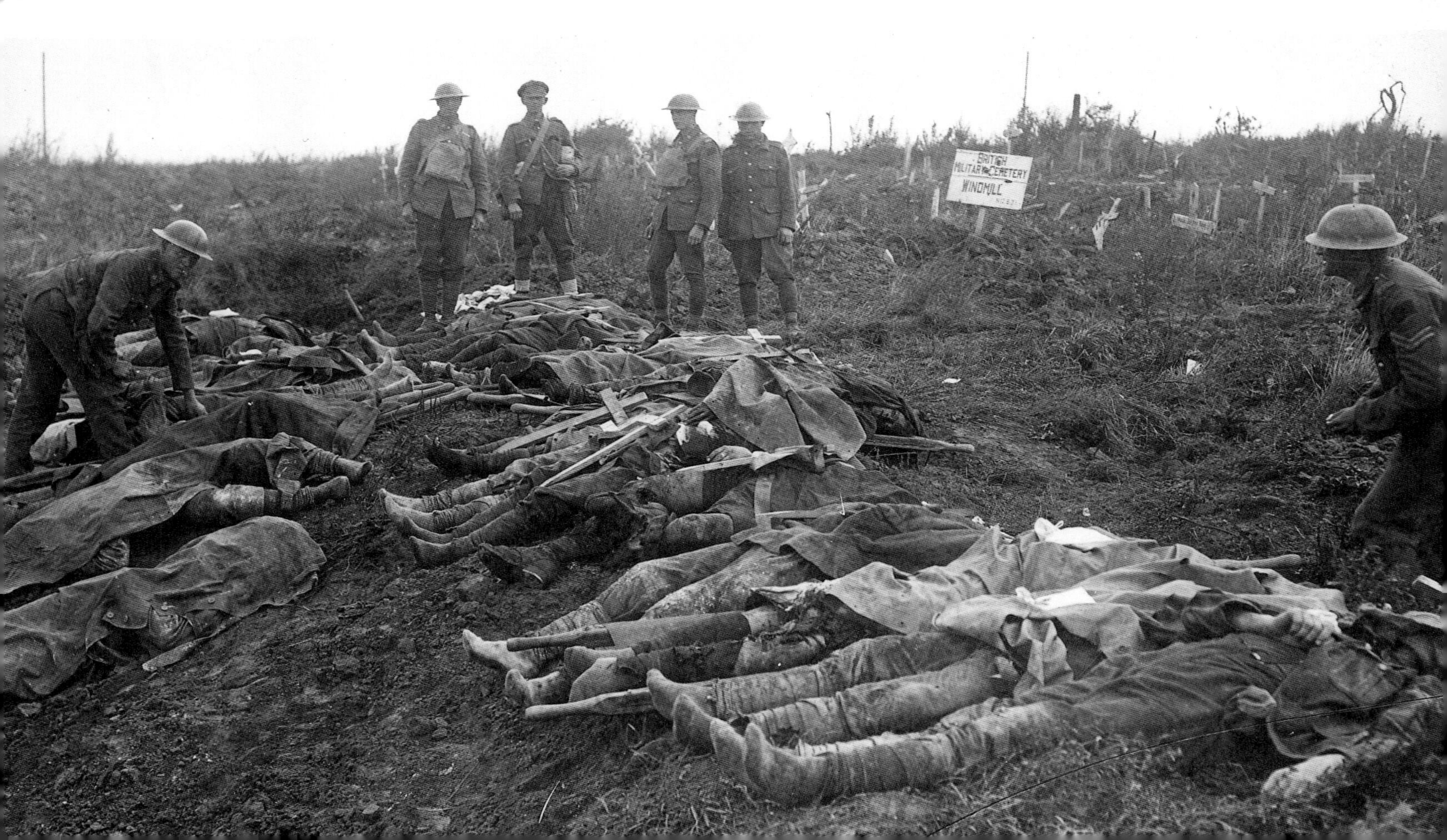
BRITISH
MILITARY CEMETERY
WINDMILL

7788

9380

Left: German soldiers rest before resuming the counter-offensive in Flanders, 1918.

Bottom left: German artillerymen of the Punt Battery pictured on one of their mighty 38 cm guns, second only to 'Big Bertha' in destructive battlefield potential, Western Front, May 1918.

Right: Field Marshal von Hindenburg (left) with First Quartermaster General Ludendorff, pictured in May 1918. The wide-ranging authority of this duo over matters military and civilian (including industry and commerce) made them *de facto* rulers of Germany.

Below: A German field gun crew in action in the Champagne, their weapon pictured at full recoil.

Bottom, far left: German soldiers haul a 7.6 cm *Minenwerfer* (trench mortar) to a new position on the front line.

Bottom, left: Field Marshal von Hindenburg, pictured on the Mole at Zeebrugge.

Bottom: M Clemenceau, General Sir Douglas Haig and M Pichon pictured before the Inter-Allied Conference at Versailles, 2 July 1918.

Bottom: The Paris Gun, seen here in action, was a long-range version of 'Big Bertha' designed as a terror weapon and aimed at Paris from a 120km distance. Its 120kg shells which took five minutes from muzzle to impact caused the deaths of 256 people between March and August 1918, but far from cowing the French seemed to stiffen their resolve.

Below, main picture: German stormtroopers in action, 1918. Elite forces who used their initiative when separated from their officers, they were first used at Caporetto where their success was notable. But their privileges including a larger ration allowance caused morale problems elsewhere in the ranks.

Top left: Major W G 'Billy' Barker, commander of No. 28 Squadron Royal Flying Corps, beside his Sopwith Camel. Once an infantryman with the Canadian Mounted Rifles, he exchanged life in the trenches for the war above.

Bottom left: British RE 8 reconnaissance bombers lined up by a roadside near Albert during the First Battle of Bapaume, 25 March 1918.

Above: A Bristol F2B Fighter of No. 139 Squadron, Italy, 1918. Powered by a 275 hp Rolls-Royce Falcon III engine, the immortal 'Brisfit' served the Royal Flying Corps/Royal Air Force in numbers: over 3100 were built and proved Britain's outstanding contribution to Allied air power.

Right: Major Raoul Lufbery of the Escadrille Lafayette. One of the few foreigners to become a French Army officer, he fell in air combat late in the war as the French-American unit's highest-scoring ace.

C1106
Y
M
C 8846
D 6894
C 8847
C 8841
C 6458
B 8254

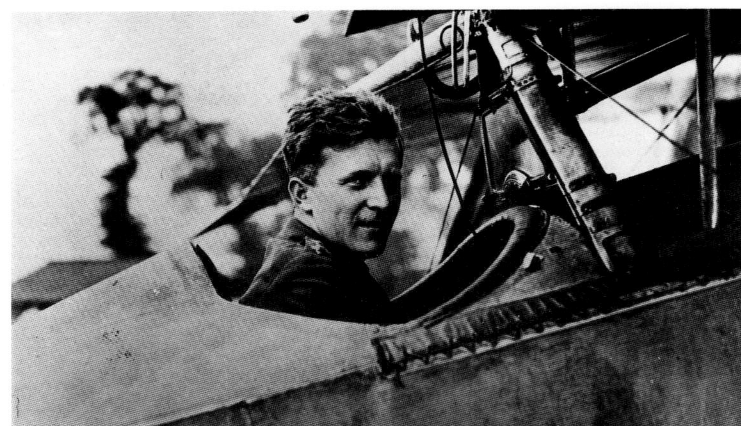

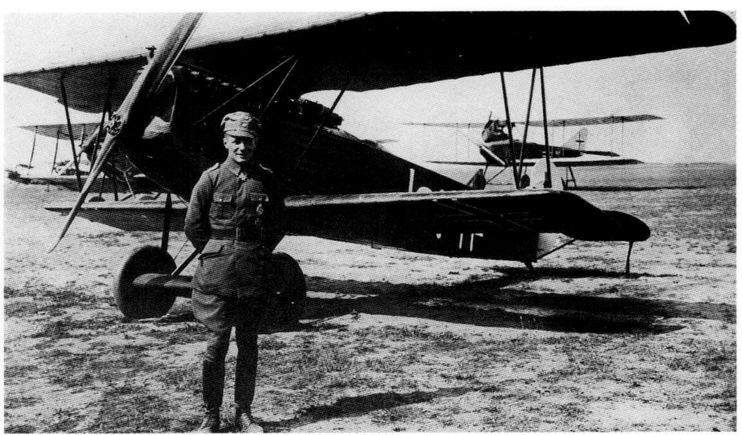

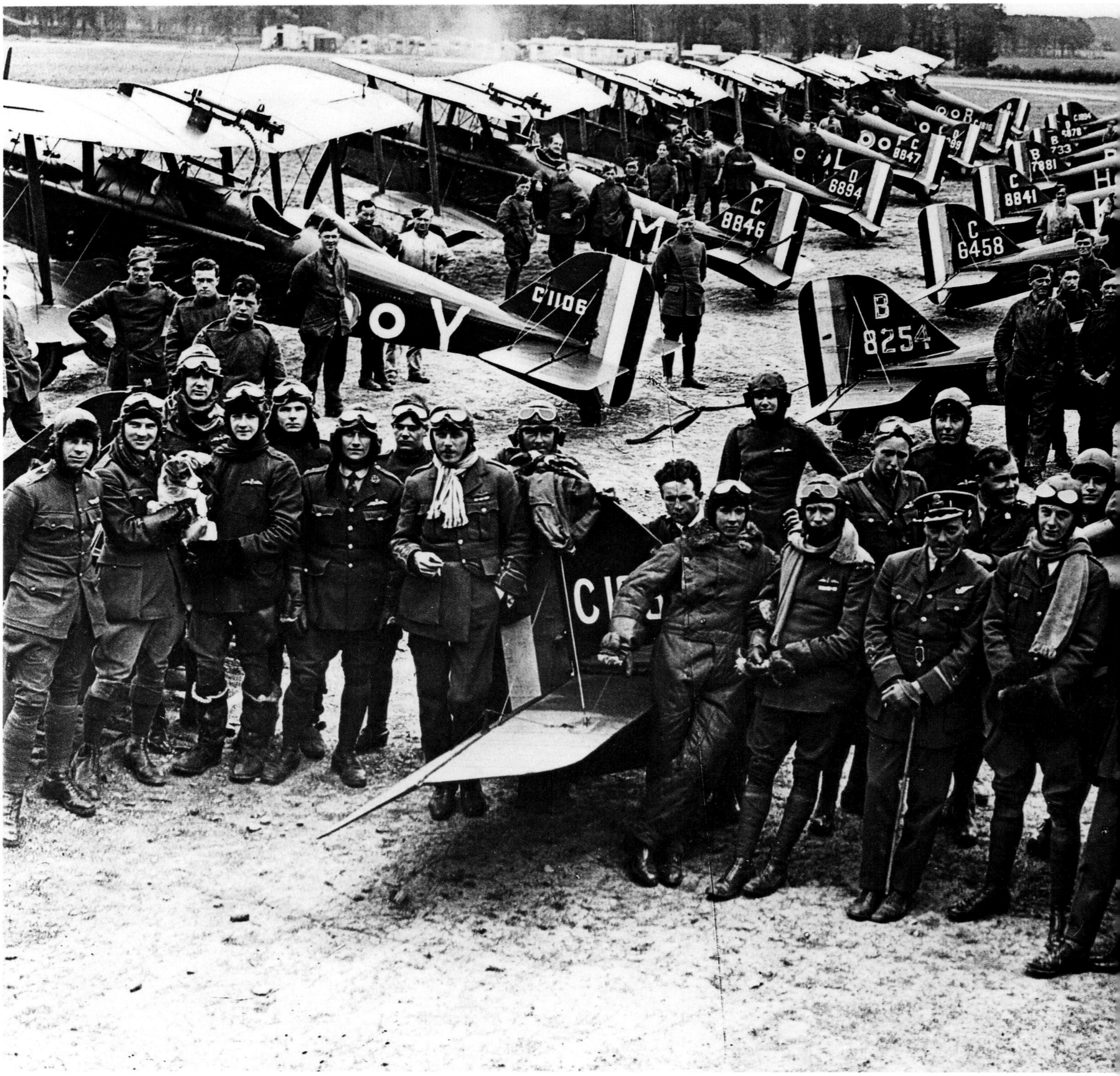

Far left: Captain William 'Billy' Bishop, a Canadian with the RFC, was the top British Empire ace with 72 victories.

Left: Oberleutenant Ernst Udet with his Fokker D VII, the machine bearing his personal distinguishing mark 'Lo'.

Top right: A mosaic of aerial photographs is assembled in a Royal Flying Corps Office near Arras, 22 February 1918.

Bottom left: Officers and SE 5A scouts of No. 1 Squadron at Clairmarais Aerodrome near Ypres, 3 July 1918.

Bottom right: Best-known as Hitler's second in command in World War II, Hermann Goering commanded JG 1, the 'Richthofen Squadron', during the first conflict.

Top right: A Bristol Fighter of No. 22 Squadron, RAF, at Agincourt, July 1918. The Squadron improvised the mounting for the top Lewis gun.

Right: Lewis guns and Lewis and Vickers ammunition are issued to observers and pilots of No. 22 Squadron at the airfield at Vert Galand, April 1918.

Below: The Fokker D VII single-seat fighter, the most capable of all German scouts, was powered by a 180 hp Mercedes engine. The type's outstanding flying qualities brought it much success in the final year of the war.

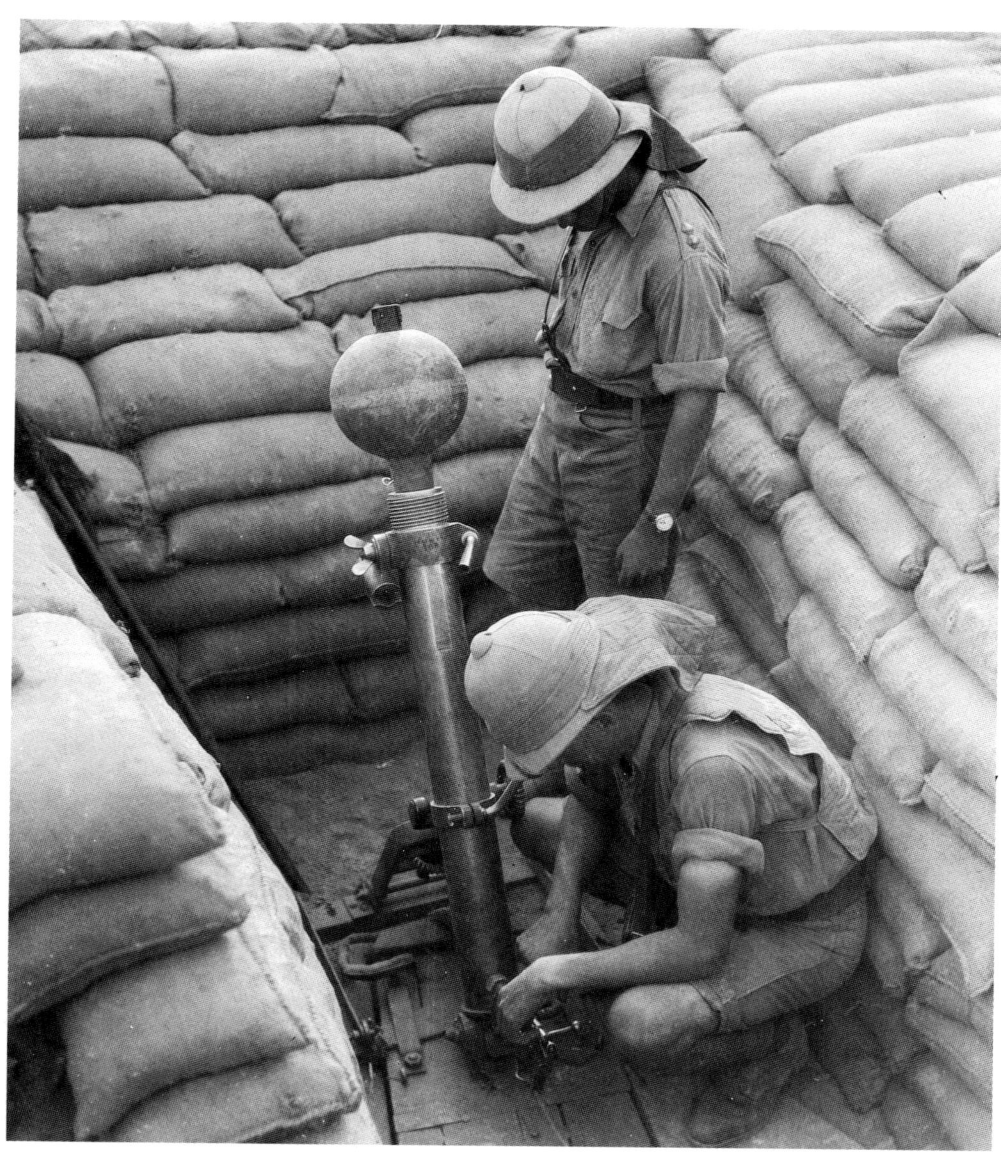

Left: British troops in Palestine prime a trench mortar in a sandbag position.

Below: Turkish troops surrender after the action at Tuz Khurmath, 29 April 1918, to men of the 38th Lancashire Brigade.

Left: The charge of the 2nd Lancers at El Afuli on Friday 20 September 1918, as depicted by war artist Thomas Cantrell Dugdale (1880-1952).

Bottom left: Sandbag defenses on the coast held by the 2nd Battalion Black Watch from the action of Arsuf on 8 June 1918 until the end of the month.

Right: General Sir Edmund Allenby, who moved from the Western Front to Palestine late in the war. His air force and cavalry turned the Turkish retreat into a rout.

Below: An SE 5A of No. 111 Squadron stationed in Palestine, where it carried out fighter and reconnaissance duties during 1917-18.

Left: The aftermath of the Battle of Sharon, September 1918, which saw 1200 Turkish prisoners taken by the Desert Mounted Corps. They are pictured while being escorted into captivity.

Bottom left: British troops take over a Turkish 7.7cm field gun five minutes after the Turkish surrender. The gunners, pictured far left, look on.

Top right: A British aircraft sets out on a scouting mission from its base in Palestine.

Bottom right: The camp and horse lines of 'A' Squadron of the 9th Australian Light Horse Regiment in a valley near Jericho, August 1918. Australian riding skills proved invaluable in Palestine.

Left: Gurkha troops are pictured at an advanced line of trenches they have just captured from the Turks.

Top right: Turkish Camel Artillery shell British armored cars on a reconnaissance mission near Kirkuk in Iraq. Fighting carried on right to the end in certain sectors.

Right: Indian troops are landed on the right bank of the Tigris, not far from the firing line in Mesopotamia. River boats like this one were in short supply for troop carrying, however.

Below: A British artillery battery and observation post on the Mesopotamian plain. The observer on the left-hand platform was provided with a shield as some concession to protection against small arms fire, but with shot falling up to 10,000 yards away such elevated platforms were essential to gauge accuracy of aim.

Left: A British river boat pictured in action against Turkish positions on the banks of the Tigris. Note the flat-bottomed boat's shallow draft.

Right: The forward gun of HMS *Sedgefly* at full recoil. These boats proved invaluable both as artillery platforms and troop transports during the campaign in Iraq.

Below: A caterpillar tractor hauls an artillery train, witness to the importance of efficient transport in the Palestine sector.

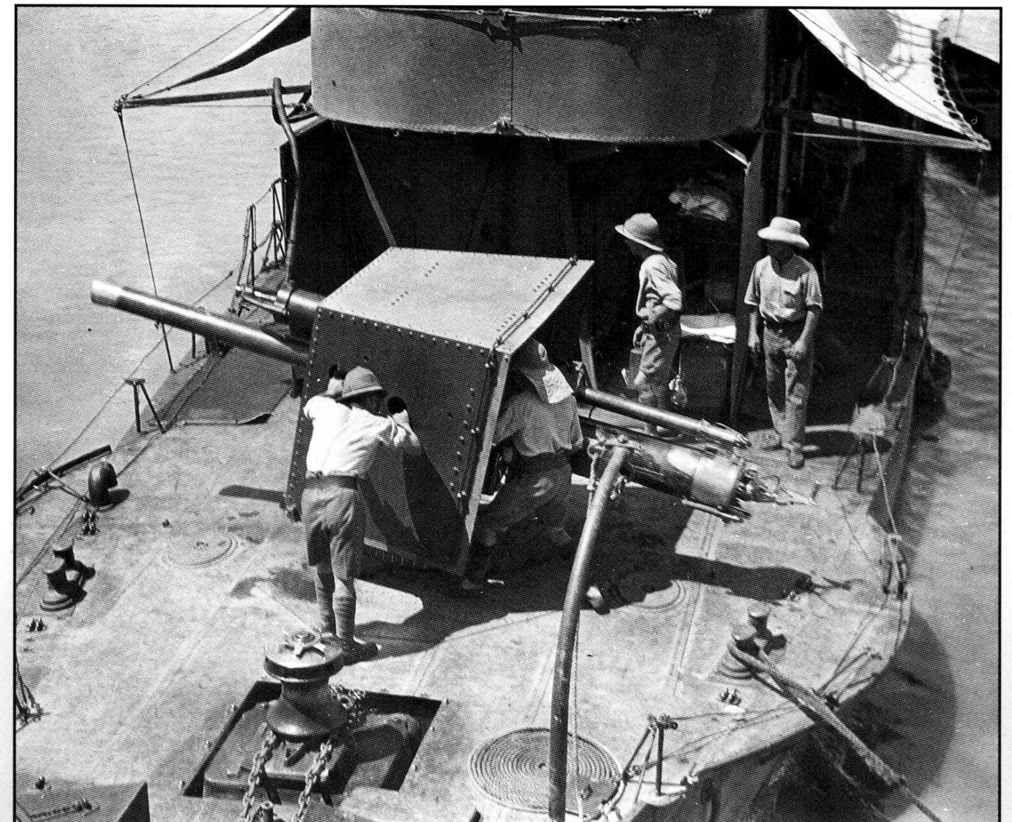

Far right: Admiral Sims and officers at Admiralty House, Queenstown, Ireland. Before the war Sims had led a great improvement in the gunnery standards of the US Navy. When the US entered the war he commanded the fleet sent to help the British.

Right: Italian motor launches at Venice.

Above: This photograph, taken from an Austrian plane, shows the Austro-Hungarian battleship *Szent Istvan* sinking after being torpedoe by Italian Motor Torpedo Boats *MAS 15* and *2*, off Premuda Island, 30 miles south of Pola, 10 June 1918.

Below: Ships of the *Orion* class in the Moray Firth, with US ships in the background. The US sent a strong squadron of modern battleships to join Beatty's Grand Fleet, confirming that body's massive superiority over its potential German opponents.

Left: The British battleship *Royal Sovereign* fires her 15-inch guns.

Bottom left: HMS *Verulam*, one of the Royal Navy's new 'V&W' class, pictured during trials in 1918. Although British sea power saw little action after Jutland, the modernisation process continued in order to maintain the Royal Navy's pre-eminent role.

Top right: Pictured here on take-off, a Sopwith Pup piloted by Squadron Commander E H Dunning subsequently made the first ship landing on the deck of the British aircraft carrier *Furious* on 2 August 1917, thus heralding the birth of naval aviation.

Right: The *Furious* was originally built as a battlecruiser but was designed with far too little armor as war experience proved. She was soon converted to the aircraft carrier configuration shown. Some months after Dunning's pioneering exploits, Camel scouts took off from the vessel to bomb the Tondern airship sheds on 19 July 1918 – the first ever carrier strike.

Below: A British monitor. Mounting large-caliber guns on a modest displacement and draft, these ships were employed for shore bombardment.

Below: British blockships in the harbor at Zeebrugge after the raid on 22/23 April 1918. One of the most important German submarine bases was at Bruges (reached from Zeebrugge) and this was an attempt to block it.

Right: Aerial view of the entrance to the Bruges Canal at Zeebrugge, showing the sunken *Thetis, Intrepid* and *Iphigenia*, and a dredger at work.

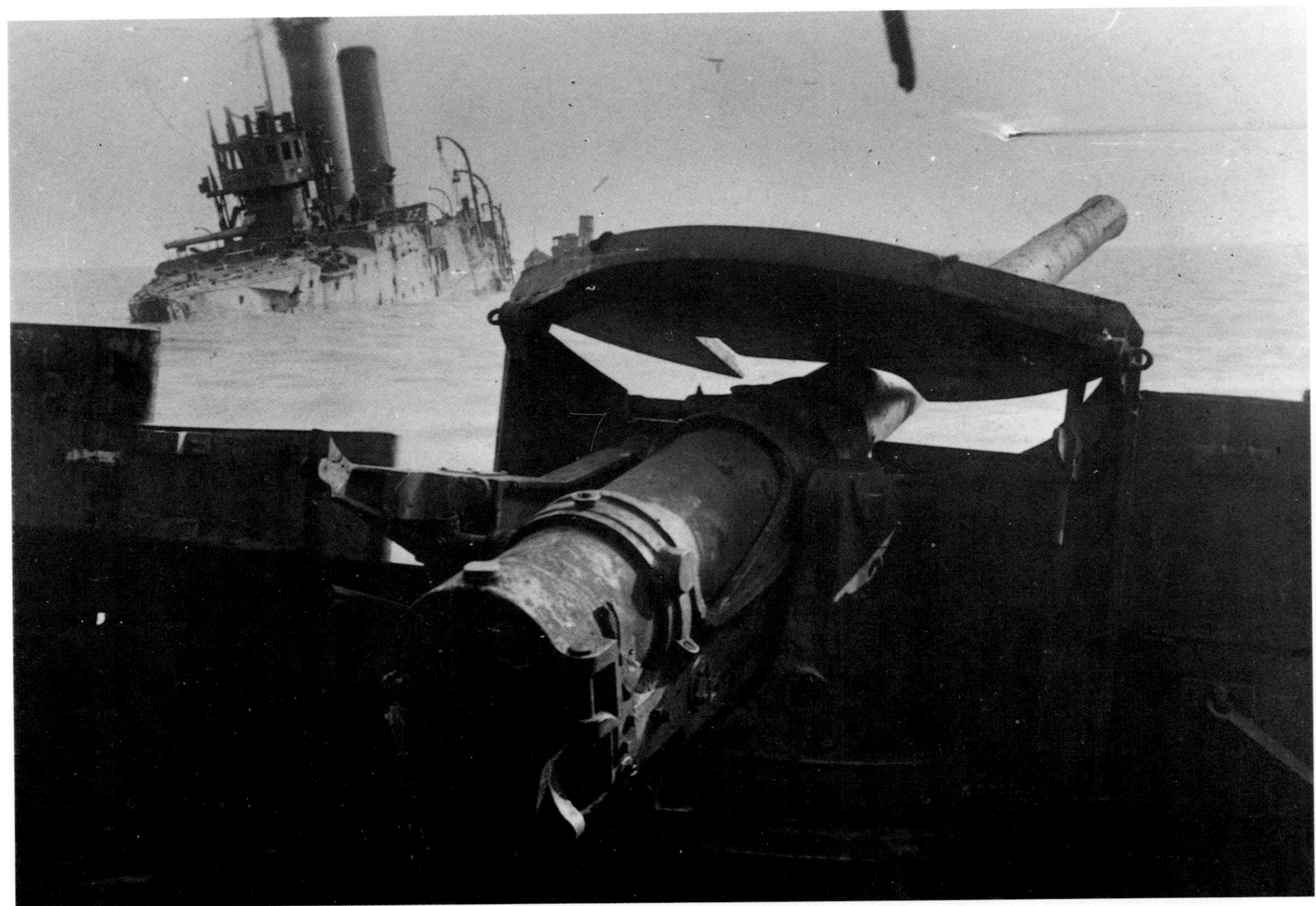

Right: A black regiment of the US 93rd Division is pictured in the trenches at Maffrecourt, May 1918. The US Army was racially segregated in World War I. The US Army began its important contribution to the Allied war effort during the later stages of the German Aisne-Second Marne offensive.

Below: Shoes worn out by troops at the front are stockpiled at a salvage depot at Tours, March 1918.

Top left: 'On the trail of the Hun', a front-line scene as depicted by war artist W J Aylward.

Bottom left: American artillery passes through a French village. Despite President Woodrow Wilson's 14-point peace plan announced in January, American troops arrived in numbers during the war's last year to help settle matters.

Top: US troops escort captured Germans through a bomb-damaged French village, 1918.

Above: An American ammunition wagon stuck in the road holds up the advance of a whole column at Beaumont Ridge during the capture of the St Mihiel salient by the US First Army, 15 September 1918. This was the Americans' first great victory and gave notice that they were a force to be feared.

Above: Sergeant Alvin C York on the hillside where he made his raid. Sergeant York won the Medal of Honor in this famous exploit and is pictured on the scene in 1919.

Top right: An American artillery battery in action near Lenoncourt on the Meuse.

Top far right: King George V inspects troops of the American II Corps with Generals Bliss and Pershing, 6 August 1918.

Top extreme right: French meets American as Marshal Ferdinand Foch (left) meets the recently-arrived General Pershing at US headquarters at Chaumont.

Below: US tanks roll into action in the Argonne Forest. Many American tanks were built in France by Renault.

Top left: This evocative illustration 'Machine Gun Emplacement' by war artist Henry Dunn juxtaposes two images of death – the gun and the gravestone. Such was the horror of World War I that it was declared 'the War to end all Wars'.

Left: An American 'doughboy' – so-called because of the dumpling-shaped brass buttons on their tunics – in action in the streets of Chateau Thierry.

Above: US troops with a Stokes trench mortar, a weapon that boasted an 800-yard range.

Top right: Hand-to-hand combat as US Marines, bayonets fixed, over-run a German machine gun post.

Right: Coast artillery at Bategcourt in the shape of a 14-inch railway gun fires on German targets fully 20 miles away, September 1918.

Right: US troops practice warfare tactics in a training area behind the lines. With their buoyant morale, their arrival was the final nail in the coffin for German hopes of victory.

Below: A US Marine machine gun detachment parades prior to embarking for the Western Front at Quantico, Virginia.

Left: Italian mountain troops or Alpini pictured in the snow on Monte Nero, near Caporetto.

Below: General Franchet d'Esperey, on landing at Constantinople, inspects the 122nd French Regiment, 8 February 1919. Franchet d'Esperey commanded the forces at Salonika in the final successful months of the war.

Bottom: Armenian troops perform drill exercises at Baku, where a German-Turkish offensive was threatened against the oilfields.

Top left: Italians attack. In October 1918 the Allied forces in Italy attacked in the Battle of Vittorio Veneto, hastening the overall Austrian collapse.

Left: A French soldier of the Corps Expeditionaire d'Orient peers over the top of a communications trench at Salonika. The collapse of Bulgaria in late 1918 left Constantinople open to the Allied advance from Salonika.

Below: German troops examine a Russian armored car captured from the Bolsheviks. By early 1918, the two sides were negotiating for peace but over one million German soldiers needed elsewhere remained in Russia.

Right: Serbian Divisions enter Monastir as they return to rid their homeland of the Austro-Hungarian invaders.

Bottom right: Austrian forces retreat across a bridge over the River Tagliamento in the very last days of the Italian campaign.

Right: Italian troops march down a mountain road, 1918.

Below: A despatch rider is held up by an Allied sentry at a barbed-wire barricade due to a gas shell bursting nearby.

Left: A French tank leads an attack along the Marne, with infantry advancing in its cover.

Below: The Third Battle of the Aisne marked the high point of German advances during 1918. A unit of French infantry moves up to the front line as a British band rests by the roadside.

Above: A German infantryman in a forward trench sounds the warning of an Allied gas attack.

Left: A German howitzer pounds British positions, August 1918.

Top right: A trench scene, 'The Ypres Salient at Night', as depicted by Paul Nash. British troops man the trench in the foreground as starbursts of explosives light up the sky overhead.

Bottom right: A German field gun crew in action on the Western Front.

Left: A German A7V tank in action in France, June 1918. Although twice as fast as early Allied tanks, this design was cumbersome and poor at crossing trenches.

Bottom left: Canadian infantry go forward at the Battle of the Canal du Nord, 27 September 1918. Note the caterpillar tracks of tanks criss-crossing the battlefield.

Right: German infantry fight a rearguard battle against ever-increasing odds. A month of retreats preceded the eventual German defeat.

Below: German A7V tanks in action on the Western Front near Villers-Brettoneaux, June 1918. This action was the first ever in which tank fought tank. The poor-performing A7V was the only tank manufactured by the Germans, but they also used captured Allied designs.

Left: An 18-pounder gun is rushed into position and put into action by its Australian crew, August 1918, as open warfare rages on the Somme.

Below: German prisoners from the Battle of Amiens are marched in past Allied anti-aircraft guns near Mericourt-l'Abbe, 8 August 1918. Dubbed 'The Black Day of the German Army' by General Ludendorff, this battle shattered German morale.

Right: New Zealanders fire as they advance on 8 August. By the end of the first day's fighting, the Fourth Army had advanced some eight miles, killed or wounded 13,000 Germans and taken 15,000 prisoners for a loss of 17,000 Allied troops.

Bottom right: Updated Mark V female tanks drive through the key town of Meaulte, 22 August 1918, consolidating the British advance. The so-called 'female' tanks were armed only with machine guns whereas 'male' tanks also carried 6-pounder cannon.

Left: British Secretary of State for War Winston Churchill pictured in the Grande Place at Lille watching a march-past of the 47th Division as victory looms, 28 October 1918.

Bottom left: The British top brass – Commander-in-Chief Field Marshal Sir Douglas Haig (center) with (from left) Generals Rawlinson, Byng, Horne, Lawrence and Birdwood – pictured at Cambrai, 31 October 1918.

Right: British tanks and infantry guard battlefield prisoners on captured ground near Bellicourt during the successful assault on the Hindenburg Line, 29 September 1918.

Bottom right: Soldiers of a Scottish Canadian regiment, their gun muzzles fitted with wire cutters, move up in preparation for the Second Battle of Cambrai.

Top left: President Woodrow Wilson, who had delayed the American entry into the war as long as possible, reads the Armistice terms to Congress, 11 November 1918.

Bottom left: Members of the British and Imperial War Cabinet pictured at 10 Downing Street, London. British Prime Minister Lloyd George is in the middle of the front row flanked by his Canadian and Australian counterparts, Sir Robert Borden (left) and Billy Hughes.

Above: The German delegation sent to Versailles in 1919. From left to right: Professor Schücking, Giesberts, Landsberg, Brockdorff-Rantzau, Leinert, Dr Melchior.

Right: Germany is declared a republic on 9 November 1918. With their army defeated, political change was sure to follow – and the huge crowds pictured here give some indication of the public interest.

Far left: Royal Navy ratings examine the captured German mine-laying submarine *UC-5* at Temple Bar Pier.

Left: The French enter the German city of Dortmund as the days of Allied occupation begin.

Below left: The surrendered German battleship *Bayern* is scuttled at Scapa Flow, 21 June 1919.

Right: The surrender of the German Fleet, 21 November 1918. The German Navy had collapsed in mutiny and revolution during the final year of the war, only the U-boat service remaining steadfastly loyal to the cause.

Below: The Royal Navy light cruiser *Cardiff* leads surrendered German battlecruisers into the Firth of Forth.

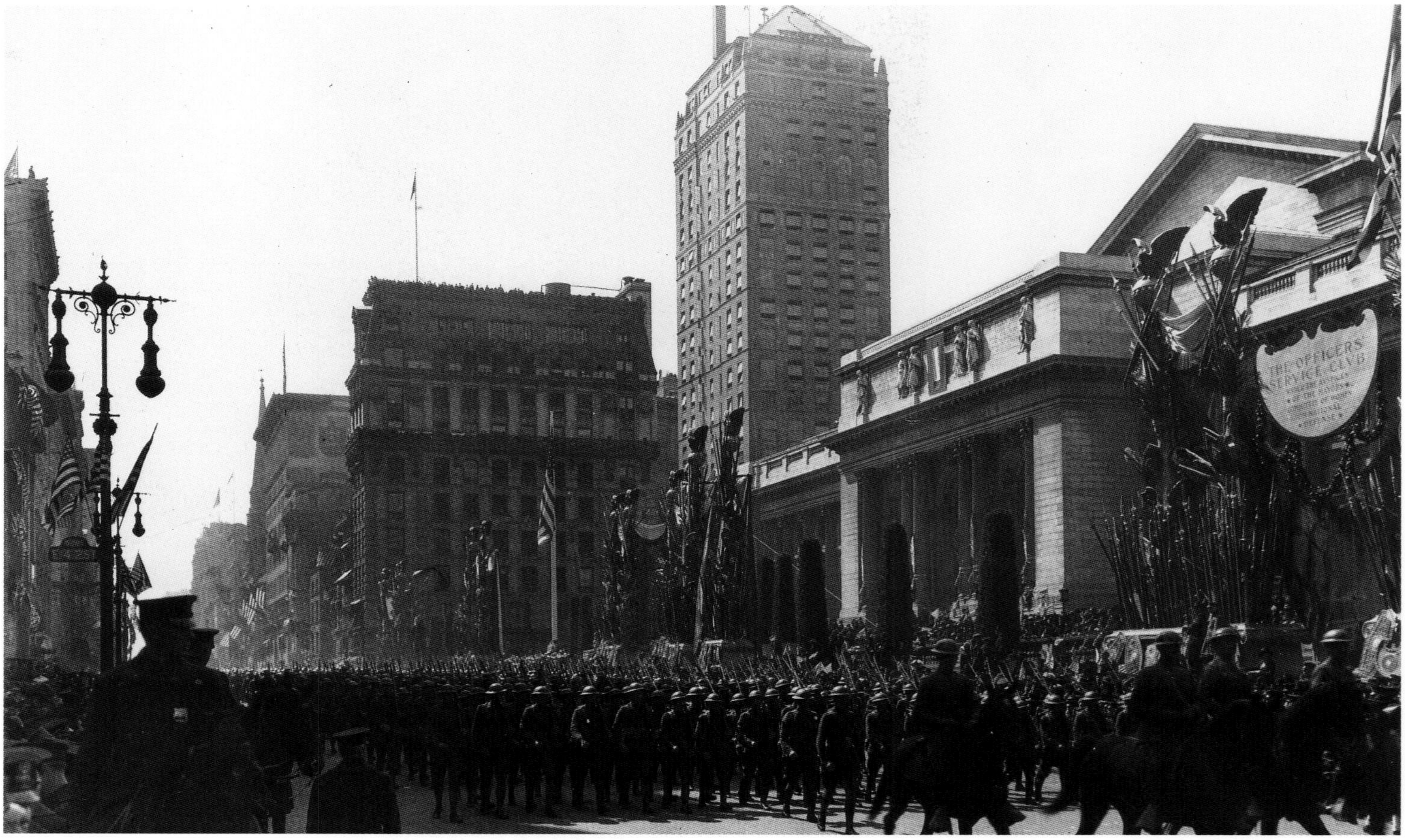
THE OFFICERS
SERVICE CLVB

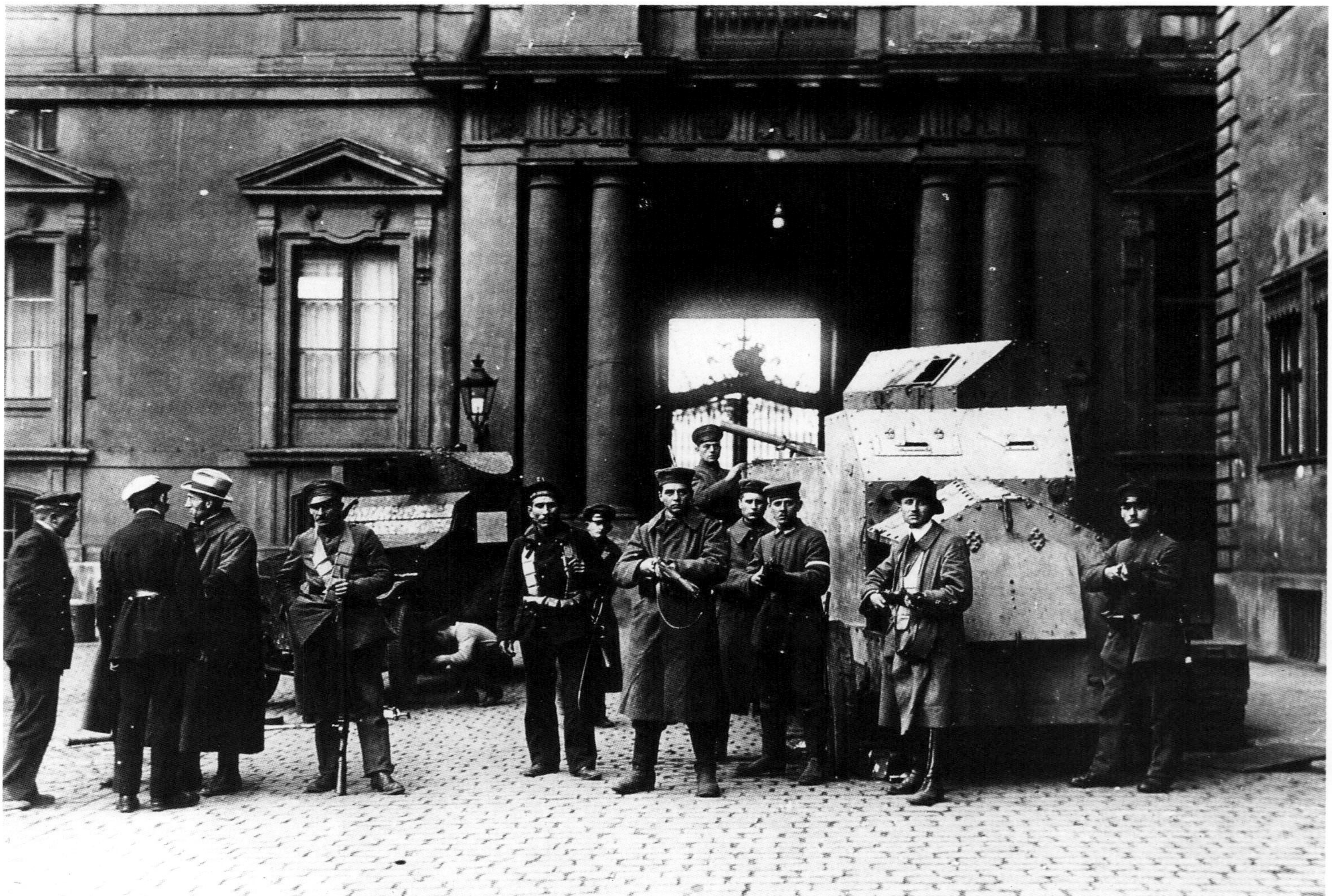

Left: The US 107th Infantry Regiment, heavily involved in the fighting that led to the breach in the Hindenburg Line, pass the New York Public Library during their victory parade.

Bottom left: The Armistice may have declared world peace, but violence and unrest were the order of the day in Germany as political factions from right and left vied for control. Ex-soldiers and their weapons were inevitably also much in evidence, as this picture taken in Berlin at the end of December shows.

Top right: An armored car and riflemen of the Soldiers' Council in front of the Berliner Schloss, 10 November 1918. The Armistice came into force at 1100 hours on the following day.

Right: The German empire may have been no more, but the peace imposed by the Allies was to be resented, then resisted by the next generation. A navy machine gun is pictured in young hands a month after the Armistice.

Below: The British battleship *Iron Duke* in action against the Bolsheviks at Kaffa Bay, 1919. Western involvement in the Russian Revolution quickly followed World War I. The *Iron Duke* had been flagship of the Grand Fleet at Jutland.

INDEX

Page numbers in *italics* refer to illustrations

Acknowledgments

The publishers would like to thank Michael Heatley who compiled the majority of captions in this book, David Eldred who designed it and Ron Watson who compiled the index. The illustrations are from the collection of the Imperial War Museum, London except for the items on the pages noted below. The publishers would like to thank all the agencies who have supplied illustrations.

Archiv Gerstenberg pages 158 top left and right, 159 bottom
Australian War Memorial, Canberra pages 78-79
Bayerische Hauptstaatsarchiv, Munich pages 289 top
WZ Bilddienst pages 140, 141 top, 192 top
Bison Picture Library pages 6-7, 16, 22(inset), 22-23, 24 top, 24-5, 29 both, 30-31, 32-3, 40-41, 42-3, 48-9, 62-3, 62 top, 63-5, 66-7, 66 top right, 68-9, 68 top, 70-1, 80-1, 82 top, 82-3, 88-9, 90-1, 92-3, 98-9, 98 top, 104-5, 106-7, 116-17, 117 top two, 120 bottom 2, 121 bottom, 112 top, 123 center, 124-25, 126-27, 127 top, 128 both, 133 center, 135 both, 136-37, 138 top, 138-39, 147 top left, 176 top, 178 both, 188-89, 217 center, 235 both, 236 top left, 236-37, 238 bottom left, 245 bottom, 244-49, 266-67, 268-69, 278 top right, 287 top, 298-89
Defense Dept, US pages 282 both
John Frost Newspapers pages 136 top right
Hoover Institute pages 15 top left, 36 bottom, 37 bottom, 155 bottom, 159 top, 236 top right
Hulton Picture Company pages 38 top, 39 bottom and top, 88 top
Robert Hunt Library pages 37 top, 94 top and bottom, 95 top right, 156 bottom, 178 top, 196 bottom right
Kriegsarchiv, Wien pages 35 top
Landesbildstelle, Berlin pages 68 top, 205 bottom
National Archives, US pages 271 top right, 275 bottom, 277 bottom, 278 top left, 278-79, 280 top left and bottom, 282 top, 283 bottom, 296 top, 300 top
National Maritime Museum, London pages 57 both, 60
Novosti pages 34 both, 64 top
Rolf Steinberg pages 15 bottom, 36 top, 43 mid right, 191 top left, 198 top
Royal Aeronautical Society pages 138 center, 141 bottom
TPS / Three Lions page 95 top
USAF pages 139 both, 144 top, 195 top
US Information Agency pages 259 bottom
Ulster Museum page 170 bottom